"There is no cause more noble than to lift the human spirit; not because we may have something to gain from it, but simply because it's the right thing to do."
- Unknown -

FOREWORD

I love storytelling. I love learning. I love watching people do what they love to do to the best of their best abilities. I love hustle. I love life on life's terms. I love struggle. I love salvation.

All of those apply to my friend John Kippen and mostly with his ability to take a very tough medical and life-changing situation and turn it into his becoming an advocate for so many who have similar or relatable experiences.

The measure of a human is what and how they take adversity and turn it into acceptance and an asset.
That's what happened here.

You learn nothing on the easy street. You learn everything when your back is against the wall and you feel very much alone.

This book is truly, the gift that keeps on giving. The gift of his experiences and his suggestions and guidelines and motivations, and that his crisis did not diminish his absolute joy of living and doing what his heart demands he do, create magical entertainment and loving support to people all over the world.

It has been my privilege to be his friend for a very long time and I am very happy to be able to introduce you to him, his life, his ideas, his struggles and his great success through this book!

Jamie Lee Curtis
ACTOR AUTHOR ADVOCATE

SAY WHAT?

"Our conference would not have been as successful without the inspiring words of John Kippen. His mix of magic, mind-reading, and storytelling stole the show!"

\- Salwa Khan -
Chief Organizer - TEDx SDSU

"I've always been fascinated by Close-up Magic. For my birthday last year, my family brought John Kippen in to entertain. He is one of the best Close-up Magicians I've ever seen!"

\- Alex Trebek -
TV Star & Game Show Host

"John is one of those rare performers who immediately makes audiences feel comfortable. We can sense that, no matter what unexpected events are thrown his way, he'll be able to handle them."

\- John Davidson -
GENII MAGAZINE

"I have been working with John Kippen as a coach for a while now. I love John's passion and ability to help me share my heart through my art... I love this man!"
- Edmund A. -

"Thank you, John, for sharing your wisdom. You have touched my heart today in letting me know that people really do care, even those you have never met before."
- Angelina H. -

"You helped guide me through some ways of thinking that have been stuck there for a long time! That unlocked something inside me that is allowing me to move forward on this path. I will never forget that."
- Magan G. -

"John Kippen has successfully taken motivational speaking and magical stagecraft to a whole new level!"
- Paul Stewart -
CEO Weekly

*"Poof! Now this is a real book of magic!
After reading John's book, you'll see how
adversity fueled both his determination and
ability to face the world. Read and you too may
dare to go where you've never gone before.
What hand do you want dealt to you?
I believe this book is a force that can change
your life and perhaps the lives of others, as it
has for John. I wish it on you. It's truly magic."*

– Robert "Bob" Fitch –
Broadway Actor & Award Winning Magician

---

*"He knows what it is like to come from a place
that is different from the rest of the world. But
this didn't stop him from achieving success
and helping others do the same."*

– Justin W. –

---

*"A very talented and amazing Magician! He will
have you in suspense and then blow your mind
with his magic tricks. He is such a nice guy too.
We had an awesome and unforgettable
experience! We highly recommend him!"*

– Meghan W. –

IN THE NEWS

"Through his book, John empowers readers to cultivate hope and fulfillment, inspiring them to navigate life's challenges with indomitable spirit and purpose. By embracing Twain's call to explore, dream and discover, he invites others to embark on a journey of personal growth and empowerment."

"It's my mission to inspire people to have the courage to be vulnerable with themselves and others," John says. "Deciding to overcome physical and emotional blockages is tough, but with the right perspective, you can quickly find joy and unlock your full potential. Remember, happiness is a choice."

This book uses state-of-the-art QR technology to enhance your reading experience, by fusing physical and virtual media.

Simply scan the codes with your smartphone camera to unlock a virtual treasure trove of fully secure, multi-media content.

If you are unable to access, or concerned with using this technology, I have you covered.

Feel free to visit the website below to access all of this book's virtual content. You will also find an appendix at the end of the book that lists the URL's for all the media.

You'll even discover a few pearls of wisdom hiding up my virtual jacket sleeve.

www.JohnKippen.com/book

ISBN #
979-8-9913776-9-0

DEDICATION

I dedicate this book to my parents, who let me follow my dreams and become anyone I chose.

To the teachers who opened my eyes to the art of out-of-the-box thinking and creative problem solving.

To my friends, who believed in me and stood by my side, through the good times and bad.

To the wonderful Jamie Lee Curtis, who believed in me even when I didn't believe in myself.

To my magician mentors, who unselfishly encouraged me to incorporate my life stories into my magic presentations.

To my audiences who, through their applause and expressions of wonder, allowed me to find joy in each and every interaction.

To my good friends, Jay Scott Berry, Romy Sperling, Robert Kezer and Georgia Scott. Without you, this book would still be just a dream.

THIS BOOK IS FOR YOU!

ACTS & SCENES

CHAPTER	PAGE

CHAPTER	PAGE

OVERTURE

Dear Friends, I invite you to join me on a journey of discovery. Life is a rollercoaster for all of us. We each face our ups and downs. In this book, you will find inspirational quotes, heartwarming stories and insightful wisdom from my life experiences. My hope is to make you cry a little, scratch your head in magical awe, and most importantly, laugh a lot.

About the title of my book.

Life is often likened to a game of cards, where the hands we are dealt can vary greatly in value and potential. Some may receive royal flushes, while others find themselves with a pair of twos. Yet, the true essence of success lies not in the cards themselves, but in how we choose to play them. *Playing the Hand You Are Dealt* is a journey through the unpredictable landscape of life, exploring the art of resilience, adaptability, and strategic thinking.

In these pages, we will delve into the experiences that shape us, the challenges that test our limits, and the choices that define our paths. Through personal anecdotes, insightful reflections, and practical wisdom, this book aims to empower you to embrace your unique circumstances and transform obstacles into opportunities.

Whether you're navigating personal setbacks, career challenges, or the complexities of relationships, the principles outlined here will guide you in making the most of what you have. Together, let's uncover the strength within you to not only play your hand, but to play it brilliantly.

Fasten Your Seatbelts...

ACT 1

Magical Beginings

"The hard must become habit. The habit must become easy. The easy must become beautiful."
- Doug Henning -

It's 6pm as I drive up to the grand entrance of *The Magic Castle*. Breathing a sigh of relief, I grab my bag of tricks from the backseat and toss the car keys to the valet. He gives me a smile and thumbs up.

I had run this routine hundreds of times by now, but tonight is special. This is, of course, no ordinary venue. *The Magic Castle* is Hollywood's exclusive private club that attracts the world's premier magicians. For over sixty years, this mystical mansion has been *"The Carnegie Hall of Magic."*

I joined the club in 2007 and began performing close-up at the tables reserved for members to entertain guests. Now, seven years later, my childhood dreams of being a professional magician were about to come true. Tonight marked my debut in the Close-up Gallery, the pinnacle of intimate sleight-of-hand artistry.

The Magic Castle

Picture Licensed through Alamy.com

I enter the ornate lobby and see friendly faces, then continue through a hidden door into the backstage of the Close-up Gallery. Carefully unpacking, I check my props and fill my pockets with the secret tools of my trade.

A knock at the door and, on cue, the porter brings in my traditional cocktail, a Diet Coke on ice and a water chaser. As I take my first sip, I wonder to myself, "How in the heck did I get here?" Through all of my life's ups and downs, from a privileged childhood, training in theater, becoming a successful tech entrepreneur, to being diagnosed with a life-threatening brain tumor which disfigured my face. I lived my life fearlessly, seizing every opportunity to step outside of my comfort zone. Through it all, I learned to find joy, and grow, from every experience, both good and bad.

I was introduced to magic by my Uncle Milton, who was a professional magician from New York City. From the age of five, every Christmas and birthday, he sent me a new magic trick. I would diligently learn the trick, and when he would come into town to visit my grandma, we would practice it together.

When I was 10, I began performing magic shows for kids in the neighborhood and at holiday functions. Uncle Milton was proud that I had followed in his footsteps and made magic my hobby.

On my 12th birthday, he came to town. I hoped he had a surprise in store for me. As I looked for a present, all I saw was a small paper envelope. With a smile, he said, "John, don't be disappointed until you open it." I tore it open to find a brunch invitation to the Magic Castle. I had heard about this mysterious place for years, but was told that it was for adults only. He explained the age limit was lowered to twelve on Sundays.

Since my 12th birthday was on a Saturday that year, he had already made reservations for the following day. For an aspiring young magician, this was the best birthday gift imaginable!

The morning could not arrive soon enough. I got up and showered, got into my dress clothes, and waited by the front window for Uncle Milton to pick me up in his shiny rented Cadillac.

I kissed my folks goodbye and hopped in the front seat. What a cool ride! As we approached, a beautiful Victorian castle glistened in the morning sunlight. It was even grander than the pictures on the invitation.

We entered the lobby and my uncle pointed to this bookcase with an owl perched on a shelf. "His name is Artemis."

I was told to whisper the magic words, *"Open Sesame,"* to the owl. With a creak, the bookcase slid open to reveal a small hallway. We immediately found ourselves in the line for the famous Close-up Gallery. We were escorted in and sat in the back row. The theater only held 24 chairs, so there wasn't a bad seat in the house. The lights slowly faded, the magician appeared and started his show. The 20 minutes passed so quickly. We gave the performer a standing ovation, and my uncle whispered in my ear, "If you keep practicing, one day maybe it will be you performing behind that table."

Hearing the sounds of the audience entering, I was jolted out of my daydream. I suddenly realized that Uncle Milton's premonition was about to come true. I break the cardinal rule of theater, and curiously peek through the curtains. I see the faces and hear the excited murmurs of the awaiting crowd. As requested, the host had selected two pretty ladies to join me at my table. I stepped back and double checked my pockets as if I was doing the Macarena. Moments later, the host asks me if I'm ready. I say, "Yes," and take a deep breath to calm my nerves.

The house lights slowly fade and the host begins, "The performer you're about to see wishes to keep his intro short so there is more time for the magic. Please welcome with a warm round of applause, John Kippen!"

I come through the curtains and take my seat behind the revered green felted table. I calmly smile and survey the crowd. Even though it's a Monday night, it's standing room only. I begin as I always do by saying, "Ladies and Gentlemen, my name is John. Welcome to my show."

"I would like to tell you a bit about me. I was first introduced to magic at the age of 5 when my uncle Milton pulled a quarter from inside my right ear." I proceed to show my hand empty and pull a silver half dollar from the ear of the assistant seated to my right. "Inflation, you know," and the audience laughs.

One of my favorite original routines is my Star Trek illusion, where I dematerialize a signed playing card from the deck through the transporter and then visually it materializes face up in a deck held by a volunteer.

Picture by Taylor Wong - Magic Castle Photographer

I welcome you all to transport to the beginning of my story. I hope you have as much fun reading it as I did living it.

- 7 -

ACT 2

Born on the 4th of July

"Time has a way of demonstrating that the most stubborn are the most intelligent."
- Yevgeny Yevtushenko -

Have you ever heard of Curious George? Well, get ready to meet the one and only Curious Kippen!

On July 3rd, 1965, my parents were enjoying a day at the Santa Anita Racetrack. My mom had been advised by her obstetrician to prepare for my imminent arrival any day. Around 4 PM, her water broke. My dad quickly found a pay phone and called her doctor, who instructed them to head to Glendale Memorial Hospital, just a few miles away.

During my mom's last ultrasound, the doctors indicated that a natural delivery would not be safe for her, as I was a sizable baby and she had a petite frame. Once they arrived, my mom was prepared for a cesarean section. As the doctor came in, she was handed paperwork to sign ahead of the scheduled surgery at 6 PM. However, my mom hesitated, wanting me to be born on the Fourth of July, not the Third.

From what I gathered, the doctor was quite frustrated with the delay and tried to persuade my mom that for her safety, they should proceed sooner. But my mom was known for her stubbornness.

My dad stood by her side, supporting her decision, and the surgery was postponed. As a result, my birth certificate proudly states that I was born on July 4th, 1965, at 12:01 AM. I truly am a firecracker baby!

Growing up with two legal eagles as parents, I was destined for a childhood filled with adult conversations and legal lingo at the dinner table. While most kids might follow in their parents' footsteps, I decided early on that law wasn't my cup of tea. But hey, I did pick up some lawyer-like thinking skills!

With dreams as big as the sky, my dad always nudged me to tackle challenges like a champ. And let me tell you, family dinners were like crash courses in legal jargon!

At the tender age of four, they enrolled me in a private school. The school motto "College begins at two." They called me a "Lifer" as I stayed at that school through graduation. This prestigious school also attracted celebrities to enroll their kids. I was never intimidated by the rich and famous, as I grew up with many of their kids.

In a sea of forty kids, my graduating class was as cozy as a family reunion. We may have been a small bunch, but we sure knew how to dream big!

Being a Buckley School student had its perks, thanks to the posh crowd and their generous tech donations. Computers waltzed into my life early on, around the 7th grade.

My Parents Fran & Hal Kippen

Picture me tinkering with an ancient Altair, punching in data on clunky cards, and dabbling with a couple of Apple II's. Then, bam! The school scored a cutting-edge DEC pdp11 - a beastly mainframe with a squad of terminals and printers.

I dove headfirst into programming with Basic and Pascal, realizing the magic of making machines dance to my tune with a sprinkle of creativity and a truckload of trial and error. It was all about turning the impossible into possible - a mantra that still echoes in my journey.

One holiday season, my folks popped the big question: "What do you fancy for Christmas?" Without skipping a beat, I blurted out my wish for a set of manuals for that brainy computer system. The catch? The price tag was a hefty $300 - a splurge for a festive gift.

Despite my struggles with dyslexia, back then when it was dubbed a learning disability, my folks took a leap of faith. They hoped those manuals would crack open the door to a world where reading wasn't a chore, but a joy.

I was like a tech Sherlock Holmes, diving deep into those manuals, unlocking the secrets of the computer system. With a dash of curiosity, and a sprinkle of mischief, I pondered what passwords my classmates would choose.

Not to play spy games, but to unravel the mysteries of social engineering. Blame it on binge-watching *Mission Impossible*, my mind was on a thrilling rollercoaster ride.

One fateful day, on page 345 of the admin guide, I stumbled upon the Money command. It was a goldmine! Fast forward to my next visit to the computer lab, waiting for the stars to align. As luck would have it, a phone call sent my teacher out of the room. It was now or never. With trembling fingers, I sat at her terminal, my heart racing. Without a second thought, I entered the command that would change everything. "Run $money > 100,40." And just like that, a cascade of usernames and passwords flooded the screen and saved to a text file in my account. But then, a twist in the plot emerged.

Once upon a time in tech land, a tricky question popped up during my sneaky escapade - a question not covered in the manual! With the teacher's return looming, I faced a split-second decision: "reset the audit trail, y/n?" Feeling the pressure, a coin toss decision led to a fateful yes, clearing the screen before a hasty print and dash home. Little did I know, that yes triggered an email confession to the administrator account. Oopsie daisy!

Back at home, amidst the crumpled printout, a shocking discovery awaited - classmates using pet names as passwords and the teacher's choice of qwertyuio and werererer. Seems like a blast from the past when hacking was a distant worry! Lesson learned: no mix of upper and lower case or punctuation, just a keyboard dance of consecutive letters. Oh, the joys of password security!

After a few days, I waltzed into computer class and took my seat at the terminal. The teacher was standing behind us, eyeing the back of our heads.

As I fumbled with the login, the password prompt kept rejecting me. Completely forgetting my hacking shenanigans, I innocently blurted out, "I can't login" The teacher's response? "Oh, John, I know. I switched things up for you and changed your password." "Alright, spill the beans, what's my new password?" She sauntered over and slipped me a piece of paper with a single word on it: "Thief." "And yes, remember to capitalize that T."

I was more than a little miffed. I swiftly tried to break into all the admin accounts, only to find she'd locked me out of everything except for the mysterious account 1,1 - the master admin that wasn't even on the official list, being the root password. I recalled the stern warning in the manual about changing this default password as one of the first tasks of being an admin.

Had she overlooked this crucial step? With a daring move, I punched in the default password for the root account. Bingo! I was back in with full admin privileges. A quick command revealed all the logged-in accounts, including the teacher's. In a mischievous moment, I reset her password and booted her out of the system. Call it a strange impulse to show off my tech prowess and stir up some fun.

Minutes later, the room filled with the frantic clatter of keys from behind me. She was furiously attempting to regain access. Each failed attempt echoed louder and louder, her fingers drumming out a symphony of password woes.

From the shadows of the classroom, a voice boomed, "John, did you change my password?" Sheepishly, I admitted, "Guilty as charged!" Her response? A poker-faced, "Changed it to what?" Trying not to burst into laughter, I muttered, "GOD." That led to an instant class dismissal and a one-way ticket to the book room for a date with the principal.

I twiddled my thumbs under the watchful eye of the tennis coach. After a two-hour wait, I was summoned to the principal's office, where my parents and my fiery teacher were ready to pounce. She envisioned me hacking the grades, but little did I know they printed report cards using that system! A week's suspension and a scolding later, I left with my folks. Dad's arm draped over my shoulder, he whispered, "Proud of you, son. Just, no more of that, okay?"

That incident sums up my bond with my parents - they knew I was a brainiac but my mischievous ways sometimes led me astray. It wasn't the first time my inquisitiveness landed me in hot water, and spoiler alert, it won't be the last. Living by the motto "Ask for forgiveness, not permission" has scored me some grand adventures, but sometimes I toe the line a bit too much. Lesson learned!

 ## Musical Memories

At Buckley, we had a music appreciation class. Hanging around the room were posters of all of the typical band and orchestra instruments. One day, David Salley, the newly hired music and theater teacher, came in and said he was starting the first Buckley School marching band. Those interested were asked to pick an instrument from the posters and he would facilitate ordering them.

Being a gadgeteer, I picked the one with the most buttons and levers, the oboe. When it arrived, I discovered it had two reeds and was a very difficult instrument, and not a common one in a marching band. I immediately ordered a clarinet. With excitement, I asked my parents to line up lessons for me at a local music shop called Baxter Northrup.

During my first lesson, I was actually able to make sound come out that sounded more like a note then a squeak. I quickly learned how to read music and would practice every night after dinner. At the first band rehearsal, I was able to play the theme from the *Pink Panther* and a march or two. I really loved playing the clarinet and made great progress.

A few weeks later, the band uniforms arrived and we went up to the football field and started learning how to march. I was assigned first chair clarinet, which meant when the conductor was not there, I would help tune the other players and start the rehearsals. Our goal was to someday march in the annual Tournament of Roses Parade. Because the school was small, we only had about 20 members in the band, so unfortunately we never made it to the parade. We did make it to every home football game and played from the stands.

The theater program at Buckley was also run by David Salley. Every spring, there would be a musical where the school would hire a professional orchestra to play the score. My playing got to be good enough that I was invited to play 3rd chair clarinet for *The King and I* musical. There was one part of the score in which I had a solo. It was a simple low set of notes, but it was a solo. I practiced until I had my part down.

I remember sitting next to Kurt, the lead clarinetist. He had a stand that held his clarinet as he played the flute and saxophone. The stand had a spot for an extra clarinet, so I asked if I could rest my clarinet next to his.

David Salley

He said sure. During the two dress rehearsals I played my part to perfection. Mr salley would point at me when it was time for my short solo and I played it like a pro.

On opening night, right before intermission, Kurt leaned over and asked if I had seen his mouthpiece cover. I said that I hadn't. As it got time for my solo, I had my clarinet in my mouth ready for my favorite part. Mr. Salley pointed to me and I blew. No sounds came out. He looked at me, with an emphatic wave of his baton, cued me again. Again, nothing came out. I was so embarrassed! The rest of the score, I had no trouble playing so I had no idea what was wrong.

At the of the end of the musical, I broke apart my instrument and put it back in the case. I was able to solve two mysteries. I looked in the bell of my clarinet and wedged in it was Kurt's mouthpiece cover. He had a habit of putting the cover on the extra stand. I guess when I put my clarinet on that peg, the mouthpiece cover got wedged in the bell. This explained why the higher notes came out just fine, but the really low notes couldn't play. Lesson learned; always check your pegs. The final three performances went off without a hitch.

Ron Neil, John Kippen & Douglas Chan

At the end of each school year, there was an award presentation. I received "Player of the Year" two years in a row. My parents were very proud.

 Bullies

I believe at some point, we've all faced bullying. I vividly recall being targeted by Brian and Jeff, two older boys from my street. After school, I would ride my bike around the neighborhood and as soon as they spotted me, they would rush out and chase me while shouting. In those moments, fear would take over, and I would pedal home as fast as I could, hiding inside. From my window, I would watch them laugh and celebrate their ability to make me feel miserable. Thankfully, this didn't happen every time I encountered them, and I could never quite understand what triggered their bullying, which continued for several years.

One Saturday morning, my dad announced that we were moving to a new house in Encino, the following weekend. When moving day arrived, I decided to face my fears for the first time. I went outside to play as usual, making sure Brian and Jeff could see me. As expected, they came out and began to chase me. My biggest fear was that, if they caught me, they would try to beat me up. However, I resolved that I was strong enough to recover from any beating they might give, so I stopped and stood my ground.

They nearly collided with me, having anticipated my flight. When they halted and saw me standing there defiantly, they were confused. After a minute or so, I could tell their game was losing its appeal for them. They shrugged their shoulders and walked away disappointed.

I went inside and shared the story with my parents. I remember asking them the rhetorical question, "Why didn't I just do that years ago?"

I learned a great lesson that day about how to stand up for myself.

The next instance of bullying occurred on the Buckley bus, involving two boys named Sean and Brad. Brad was quite short for his age and seemed to be trying to compensate for his height. Sean came from a troubled background and lived with his father. Although he was quite popular with all the girls, he had a tendency to bully others.

Unfortunately, I was on the same bus as him, as we lived just a few miles apart. One particular day, we had a substitute bus driver, and Sean seized this chance to get up and punch me on the side of my head. He struck my left ear, and it really hurt. For some reason, I had forgotten the lessons I had learned from my encounters with Jeff and Brian about standing my ground. Sean was a few years older and eventually got a car, which meant he stopped taking the bus. I focused on avoiding him on campus and waited for the day he would graduate.

Fast forward about a decade, and I recall reading in a Buckley alumni newsletter that Sean had secured a position with the Los Angeles Public Defender's office. I reminded my mom of how Sean had bullied me in high school, to which she smiled and replied, "And... why are you telling me this?" By that time, my mom had been close friends with the personnel director at the Public Defender's office for over 30 years. After persistently asking her for some form of payback against Sean, she finally agreed, saying, "Alright, I'll see what I can do." She successfully arranged for Sean's first assignment to be at Beaudry Street in downtown Los Angeles, where the most dangerous criminals were taken for court appearances. These individuals often lacked the means to hire a private attorney, so they were assigned a public defender.

Sean didn't last even a year before he decided to quit. It seems he experienced what it felt like to be truly miserable. Sometimes, karma has a way of coming full circle.

Upon reflection, I struggled if I should include this story in the book. Looking back, I realize that, as a younger man, I was impulsive in wanting to exact my payback. We all feel sleighted at certain times in our life. I now know that revenge is never the answer. Even if in the moment it does feel satisfying.

The Disappearing House

As mentioned in my introduction, my parents were true dreamers. The following story perfectly illustrates how nothing could deter them from pursuing their dreams, a core belief of theirs that has resonated with me throughout my life.

While many of my classmates resided in sprawling homes in Beverly Hills and Bel Air, often featured in architectural digest and interior design magazines, my house also made it into a national publication, though not in the way you might expect.

My parents always envisioned living in a home with a breathtaking view. After selling their first house in 1974, they began searching for something larger. We attended an open house in the Encino Hills, located at the end of a quiet cul-de-sac. Upon entering, I felt an unsettling vibe. Something didn't feel right. However, when my parents caught sight of the stunning view of the San Fernando Valley from the living room, they instantly fell in love with the house. Before I knew it, we were packing our belongings to move.

One wonderful advantage of attending Buckley was their fleet of buses. Regardless of where we lived, a Buckley bus would arrive to pick me up for school. This arrangement greatly simplified our lives, especially since both my parents were working.

At the end of February 1978, we experienced two weeks of relentless rain. On Friday, March 3, 1978, we noticed some half-inch cracks forming around the pool deck, which cantilevered over a slope leading to the houses below ours.

By Saturday morning, the cracks had widened to 6 inches. On Sunday, the entire backyard, including the recently drained pool, sank about 6 feet.

My dad reached out to a contractor client of his to assess the situation. When Earl, his client, saw the cracks, we realized something was seriously wrong. He went to his car, retrieved a crowbar and hammer, and began tearing up the living room tile. To our shock, we discovered that the cracks extended into the living room's foundation. It was clear that it was only a matter of time before the house would slide down the hill.

We contacted Jerome, another of my dad's clients, who arrived with a group of friends from South Los Angeles to help us move our furniture. Somehow, they managed to find a moving truck on a Sunday; we never asked how. My parents and I watched in awe as this supportive group moved our belongings into the truck. Anything that didn't fit was placed in the carport by the front door.

One of my most vivid memories from that day is of the volunteer's wives delightfully rummaging through our pantry, discovering gourmet ingredients, as my mom was an exceptional cook. They began preparing meals for all the volunteers, even amidst the sounds of creaking floors and breaking beams surrounding them. They turned the situation into a somewhat eery celebration.

We were kindly invited to spend the night at a close family friend's home, while Jerome offered to sleep in the truck to guard our belongings.

Around three in the morning, we received a call from the police asking if we were aware that a man was sleeping in a truck parked in front of our house filled with our furniture. We quickly confirmed that we did and requested that they leave poor Jerome alone.

As dawn broke, we headed to a local diner for breakfast and reached our block by 9 am. At the top of the one-way street, two police officers were redirecting traffic. We informed them that we lived at the end of the street, and their expressions spoke volumes. As we drove down the street, we were struck by the sight of numerous trucks. Initially, we thought the whole block was relocating. However, as we passed each truck, we noticed the logos of local TV stations stenciled on the sides.

Sunday afternoon, March 5th, we returned home to discover that the entire backyard had given way.

Soon after, we stood in the driveway in disbelief as our home split in two.

All that remained was a shell of the entrance and the view that convinced my parents to buy the house.

All reduced to a pile of rubble.

Photo Credit to my Dad and his Instamatic Camera.

We arrived at the beginning of our long driveway just in time to witness our house split in half, and within ten minutes, one side had vanished. All that remained was the breathtaking view of the city that my parents cherished so dearly, now the sole remnant of their dream home. The dramatic images captured the attention of The National Geographic magazine, featuring them in their May issue.

Later, we learned that the previous owners had sold the house without revealing that the slope had previously failed and was rebuilt. My mom said, "John, we should have heeded your warning about the house." That offered little solace.

News spread quickly throughout my school, and I became a local celebrity for about a week, as we were interviewed by several TV news programs.

For the following six months, we lived out of a couple of suitcases, moving from one friend's house to another until my parents found a new place. This one was perched on an even higher hill, boasting an even more magnificent view. My parents were determined not to let the destruction of their home dampen their dream of living with a view. Perhaps there's a lesson in that somewhere.

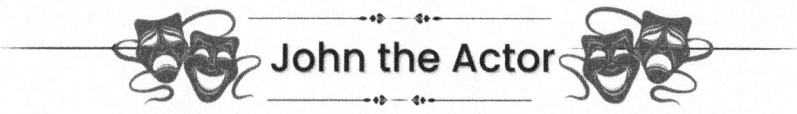

John the Actor

One afternoon I was walking across the Buckley pavilion which was a multi purpose room with a basketball court and a stage. I was heading to the band room to practice. All of a sudden Mr Salley stopped in his tracks and called my name. He was in the middle of a rehearsal for the Musical, *Annie Get your Gun*. He announced to the cast on stage that he had found his Chief Sitting Bull. I had no idea at that moment in time, my life would take a sharp turn as that became my introduction to the world of theater.

I dropped my bags and headed up the stairs to the stage. I was handed a script and told to read my lines as they rehearsed. Mr. Salley told me that I was going to be an Indian chief, and showed me how to deliver my lines. I picked it up quickly. I had a favorite line that I delivered as I put my hands around the neck of the character, Dolly Tate, played by Candace Savalas, the daughter of the great actor Telly Savalas. You remember the bald lolly pop sucking detective from the 70's show Kojak; "Tell, or I squeeze your neck, until your eyes drop on floor... like grapes."

Ron Ayala, Lisa Nelson, Bill Sanders & Chief Sitting Kippen

As the rehearsal went until around 10 pm, I got a ride home from Doug Llewellyn, a Buckley parent. The name might sound familiar to some. He was the court interviewer on the TV show, *The Peoples Court*, starring Judge Wapner. As I got out of the car at my front door, my dad came out in his bathrobe breathing fire. "Why are you bringing John home so late?" he yelled. I tried to calm my dad down and explain that theater rehearsals often went into the late evening hours. I was so embarrassed that Dad took it out on poor Doug.

I guess my new theater hobby was a shock to me and my parents. My journey continued as I either auditioned or volunteered for every production. Weekends were reserved for set building. I had experience using tools, so Mr. Salley quickly showed me the mission for that day, and off I went. Often times the task at hand was to build the set walls, or flats in theater speak.

These consisted of pieces of 1" x 3" wood laid out in a rectangle. Each corner used corrugated fasteners to hold the wood together. Small pieces of plywood, cut in the shape of triangles, were placed in each corner of the frame to give the frame structural integrity.

These plywood triangles were attached by clout nails. They got this name because it only took one clout of a hammer to seat them all the way. The next step was to cut sheets of muslin and stretch the fabric to cover the back of these frames. The muslin was stretched tight and then glued and stapled down. I had this procedure down to a tee, so Mr. Salley would send me other volunteers so that I could show them the process and make sure they were doing it carefully.

Quick note; If you use a skill saw to cut the wood, make sure you set the depth of the guide. One mistake, and you would cut a deep gouge into the very expensive gym floor. Shhhh, that can remain our little secret.

As the set began to take shape and the painting team took over, I turned my attention to hanging the lighting for the show. There was a front lighting position with a horizontal pipe to which we attached the lighting instruments.

We also needed lights coming from the side, so we raised the basketball backboards and hoops as high as they would go so that we could hang additional lights from them. I don't think the basketball team every forgave us.

Looking back, what I learned from my high school education was how to think creatively, excited for the next chapter of my life.

JOHN DAVID KIPPEN

MOM AND DAD. You have always been there when I have needed you, and have sacrificed much to make me happy. I could not have asked for better parents. Best of all, our relationship is not only one of a parent to a son, but of a friend to a friend. I will always love you very much.

MAGO. You have given me love and guidance, but more than that you have given me companionship. We have been able to talk about everything and I have learned much from you. You will always have my love.

DR. BUCKLEY, MR. BAUMHOFF, MR. ARNOLD, MRS. STROM, AND MRS. TOBOCO. All of you have helped me tremendously throughout my twelve years at Buckley. You have prepared me for more than the next four years of my life. I thank you and I will keep in touch.

MR. SALLEY. You have opened my eyes to a part of myself that I never knew. The skill of acting that you have shown me has changed my outlook of my life, and my life in general. Thank you. I will never forget you.

MR. THEPOT. Thank you for giving me the second chance I needed. I will always be grateful.

BILL SANDERS. The friendship that we have created the last few years has been a special one. Good luck in the future. Break a leg.

TO ALL OF MY TEACHERS. I have been fortunate to have had the best teachers that a student could ask for. Thank you for sharing your knowledge with me. I will use it well.

TO ALL OF MY FELLOW STUDENTS. I have learned much from you the past sixteen years and hope that our friendship's can continue for as long as we live. Keep me in your thoughts, you will always be in mine. Good luck.

TO ANYONE I MAY HAVE FORGOTTEN. I only wish to say I am sorry, and please don't forget me.

My graduation yearbook page

ACT 3

Early Celebrity Encounters

"Snatching the eternal out of the desperately fleeting is the great magic trick of human existence."
- Tennessee Williams -

As an only child, my extended family was quite small, consisting of my mom, dad, two grandmothers, a few cousins, and my uncle Milton. I shared a special bond with my maternal grandmother. When I was learning to speak, I struggled to say "grandma," and it came out as "Mago," a name that stuck with her. She was married to, my grandpa Joe, a dentist whose practice was located in the heart of Hollywood. Sadly, he passed away the year I was born, so I have no memories of him. He treated many celebrity patients, including Ben "Bugsy" Siegel and Jayne Mansfield.

Grandpa Joe was an extraordinary craftsman, known for creating miniatures of his home in the Hollywood Hills. His work was so highly regarded that pieces can be found in several museums, although most of them, ended up in my home. I believe this is where my knack for fixing and tinkering originated.

Following his passing, Mago received an invitation to move into room 501 at the renowned Sportsman's Lodge hotel, where the owner was also a former patient of my grandfather.

From my earliest memories, my dad would take me to visit Mago most Saturdays. She took great pride in me and introduced me to all the hotel staff, earning me the nickname "Little Johnny." Mago and I often enjoyed lunch together in the coffee shop. Due to the hotel's proximity to the studios, many famous individuals would stay there.

Mago gifted me a small autograph book with a cloth zippered cover, which was kept in her mailbox behind the front desk. Whenever a celebrity checked in, the hotel manager would request their signature for my book. During my visits, I had the exciting opportunity to obtain those autographs in person.

Some of the autographs include President Gerald Ford, John Wayne, Kim Novac, Dick van Dyke, Robert Wagner and Eddie Albert, just to name a few. One afternoon, Mago and I were enjoying lunch at a coffee shop when she spotted a man sitting at the counter. She encouraged me to quickly fetch my book and ask him for his autograph, mentioning that my grandmother believed he would become very famous one day. The man graciously signed my book while smiling at Mago. Upon returning to our table, I read the signature, which said, "Thanks for asking. Your friend, Marvin Hamlisch." Mago had just seen his first television appearance on the Mike Douglas show the previous day. He later composed the music for one of my favorite films, *The Sting*.

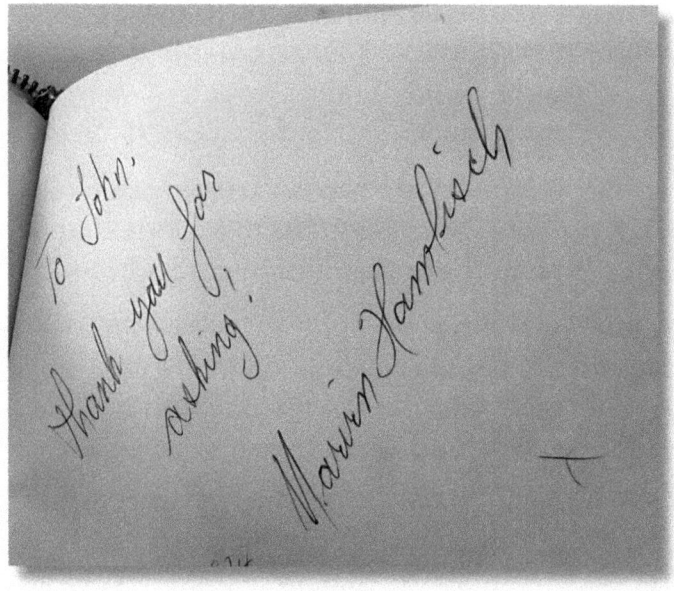

Marvin Hamlisch

Evel Knievel

During another visit to the hotel, I spotted a large semi-trailer parked in the lot. My curiosity piqued, and as I approached, I noticed the logo painted on the side: Evel Knievel. He had attempted to jump the Snake River just days earlier. As I neared the cab of the truck, I saw a round lock positioned just above my reach. Ever since I became captivated by locks and keys while watching shows like *The Rockford Files* and *Mission Impossible*, I had developed a habit of picking up any lost keys I found and adding them to my collection. I was convinced I had a key that would fit that round lock; the only question was, would it turn?

There was only one way to find out. Balancing on my tiptoes, I managed to insert the key into the lock. Unfortunately, it went in at an angle and got stuck. Panic set in as my key ring and all the keys dangled from the lock. Just as I was trying to devise a solution, a voice boomed from behind me, "What are you doing, kid?" Turning slowly and looking up, I found myself face to face with Evel Knievel himself. His frown quickly transformed into a smile as I explained, "I wanted to see if my key would work in your lock!" He retrieved my keys and, as he handed them back, said, "You sure remind me of myself at your age." He then asked if I was hungry. "Of course!" I replied.

We made our way to the coffee shop, where he treated me to a grilled cheese sandwich and fries. I dashed to grab my autograph book from the front desk. Evel gladly signed it and began sharing story after story about his daring career. He was an incredible storyteller. Perhaps it was then that I realized the magic of a good story to captivate an audience. That became one of the most exhilarating hours of my life.

About a week later, I received a call from Ross at the front desk, informing me that a large package had arrived with my name on it. During my next visit to Mago's, my dad accompanied me to discover what was inside. It was a four-foot-tall framed picture of the poster for the Snake River jump, alongside a signed photo of Evel riding his motorcycle. That picture still hangs in my den today.

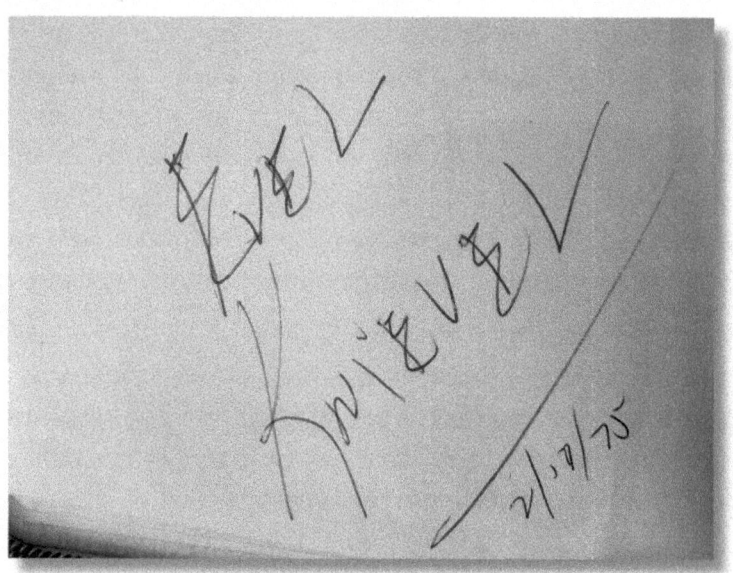

I've always experienced some oddly fortunate events. A few years after meeting Evel, Mago called me to share a shocking incident: two men had come in overnight to rob the hotel front desk. Upon finding only about $100 in the cash drawer, they decided to douse the lobby with gasoline and set it ablaze. Thankfully, the staff escaped unharmed, but the entire lobby was destroyed. The fire was so intense that it melted all the spare room keys stored in the mailboxes.

Remarkably, the only item that survived the blaze was my autograph book. Although the cover was slightly singed, the pages remained completely unharmed. I keep it safely stored in my home safe.

Picture Courtesy of Evel Knievel himself

Autograph Book Cover

Kate Smith

Dick Van Dyke

John Wayne

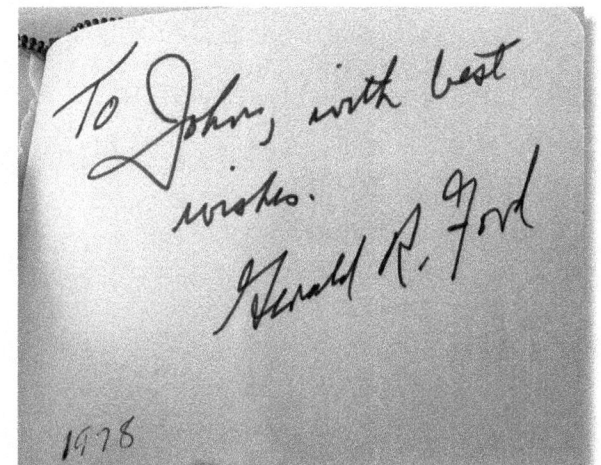

Gerald Ford

Ethel Merman

PEARLS OF WISDOM
Forgiveness

The Transformative Power of Forgiveness

Forgiveness is a profound act that can bring tranquility to our hearts. It involves releasing the anger and pain inflicted by someone else's actions. By choosing to forgive, we liberate ourselves from the weight of negative emotions. In this section, we will delve into the concept of forgiveness and explore how we can incorporate it into our daily lives.

Grasping the Essence of Forgiveness

Forgiveness does not imply that we condone someone's actions. Rather, it is about opting to let go of the pain and resentment that we carry within us. When we forgive, we not only aid the person who has wronged us; we also facilitate our own healing and progression.

Acknowledge Your Emotions

The initial step toward forgiveness is recognizing your feelings. It is completely natural to experience hurt, anger, or sadness when someone wrongs us. Take the time to comprehend your emotions—consider journaling about them or confiding in a trusted friend. Acknowledging your feelings is crucial before you can release them.

Make the Decision to Forgive

Forgiveness is a conscious choice. You hold the power to release your anger. Remember that clinging to resentment ultimately harms you. Take a moment to affirm to yourself, "I choose to forgive." This straightforward statement can initiate your healing journey.

Empathize with the Other Person's Perspective

At times, it can be beneficial to attempt to understand the situation from the other person's viewpoint. What circumstances may have influenced their actions? This doesn't justify their behavior, but gaining insight into their perspective can foster compassion. Everyone is prone to mistakes, and often, people inflict harm unintentionally.

Be Patient with Yourself

Forgiving can be challenging and may require time. Practice self-compassion and allow yourself to feel upset for a while. It's perfectly normal. Just keep in mind that you are moving toward forgiveness. Embrace your emotions while continually reminding yourself of your intention to forgive.

Emphasize the Positive

When you decide to forgive, concentrate on the positive elements of your life. Reflect on what you are thankful for, such as your supportive friends and family, your passions, or your accomplishments. Shifting your focus to the good can help facilitate the release of negative emotions.

Release the Past

Clinging to past wounds can burden us significantly. To truly forgive, we must learn to release these attachments. This doesn't imply forgetting what occurred, but rather choosing not to allow it to dictate our lives. Picture each negative emotion as a balloon, and visualize yourself letting it go into the sky, watching it drift away. This imagery can serve as a powerful representation of letting go of pain.

Seek Closure

Sometimes, the path to forgiveness involves a conversation with the individual who caused you pain. If you feel comfortable and prepared, consider discussing how their actions impacted you. Sharing your feelings can lead to closure and enable both parties to move on. However, remember that it is perfectly acceptable to forgive even if the other person isn't ready to change.

Embrace the transformative power of forgiveness and witness the changes it brings to your life.

"When you forgive, you in no way change the past - but you sure do change the future"
- Bernard Meltzer -

ACT 4

"You don't have to see the whole staircase, just take the first step."
- Martin Luther King, Jr. -

As I graduated from Buckley, I was accepted to California State University, Northridge as a Theater major. Within a week of beginning of the the fall semester, I was given the position of Prop Master for a touring production of a children's show called *Stone Soup*.

One of the props that I needed to design was a simple tripod to hang a pot of soup over a fire. I was in the scene shop with all the raw materials laid out on a workbench, but I couldn't figure out how to get started. I stood there frozen in my tracks and my instructor, Jerry Abbitt approached.

Jerry was from Paducah, Kentucky. He wore suspenders and always had a cigar hanging halfway out of his mouth. In Jerry's Kentucky accent, he said to me, "Boy, I didn't take you to raise." That was Jerry's way of saying, "What the heck are you doing?" I replied, "Jerry, I'm having trouble getting started." He immediately said, "Kippen, there you go again. You're in your head. Stop it! Just grab three sticks of wood from the workbench and tie a piece of rope at the top of the three. Then splay the wood out and tie another piece of rope around the bottom of each of the pieces. The final step, hang a hook from the top. Now you have a tripod." In a louder voice, he repeated, "Get out of your head and try things until they work." Now that was a valuable lesson! It was true. I was fearful of taking action, and for whatever reason, I was overthinking it.

Ever since, the word Tripod has served as my *Positive Trigger Word,* for anytime I was up against a seemingly insurmountable challenge. Repeating the word tripod as a magical mantra helped me get out of my head, and start trying things until a path to success materialized.

We all experience fear of challenges from time to time. Often, when we achieve the result we wanted, we comment, "That wasn't so hard after all." We now find ourselves full of pride and a sense of accomplishment.

Using our own positive trigger words can bring back those memories and feelings of triumph over obstacles. All of a sudden we have the power to take action. If your first attempt is unsuccessful, it's not a failure, it's a learning experience. The more you practice this concept, the more you can achieve.

Give it a try. What do you have to lose?

Theater

My interests moved from prop building to lighting and technical direction. I would volunteer for light hanging and focusing sessions which happened one weekend per month. There I learned the intricacies of lighting a full theatrical production. After a year of volunteering , a paid position became available called The Student Lighting Supervisor. In this job, I was responsible for supervising each production's lighting crew. Most crew members were wet behind the ears, as this was part of the Basic Lighting 101 course. It was at this point, I discovered my knack for teaching.

I became the person that the lighting crews would come to when they needed assistance. My responsibilities included helping the master electrician and lighting crew hang and focus the lights per the lighting designer's instructions. This gave me the skills to start designing the lighting for future productions. A whole new world opened up. As I started designing, I realized that I could become another performer in the production. There was no feeling like executing a lighting scene and hearing the oohs and aahs from the audience as they saw the sets and actors come alive.

The dean of the School of the Arts soon recognized my innate leadership abilities. He started a guest artist series, inviting professional actors and dance companies to perform on campus. He hired me to handle all technical aspects of the series. I had the pleasure of working with notable names like William Windom, Danny Glover, Cicely Tyson and The American Ballet Theater. The dean wanted very little to do with executing these events, besides writing the check for the performers, and showing up for the performance. I got the chance to name my price and the dean gladly paid it.

Doug Henning

One summer I received a call from the dean that a magician had rented the theater for a month to rehearse his show to take on the road. I didn't believe my ears as he told me it was the master magician, Doug Henning. I was in charge of hiring the crew that would also work the event, but I made sure that I would be Mr. Henning's assistant and right-hand man. Being an amateur magician at the time, this was an amazing and exciting opportunity.

Early Monday morning, we unloaded Doug's two semi-trailer trucks filled with illusions, costumes and props. Doug was eager to meet us and introduced his wife, Debbie, and manager, Steve Kirshner. They were all so gracious and giving. Doug immediately recognized my passion for magic and took me under his wing. I spent almost a month learning many of his secrets of magic including how he would make a car vanish on stage.

"The Art of a Magician is to create wonder. If we live with a sense of wonder, our lives become filled with joy."
- Doug Henning -

I recall, at one point, I saw a Metamorphosis Trunk in the wings. This was his famous version of the classic transformation illusion, where he and Debbie magically changed places. Being young, bold and foolish, I suggested to Steve that I could perform that illusion. Having worked in a magic shop for a couple of years as a teenager, I was familiar with the workings of the trunk. Steve said, "Oh let's see." He lifted the lid, and I got in.

Steve replaced the lid and locked me inside. As I attempted to escape, I realized there was something amiss. I quickly realized that I was trapped inside as Steve had put the lid on upside down. After about a minute, I knocked on the lid and sheepishly asked if he would please let me out. I sure learned an invaluable lesson.

As part of his show, Doug did a close-up segment, performing the famous Coins Across routine, wherein five coins invisibly pass from one hand to another. That evening, I went home and found a bunch of silver dollars and brought them in with me the next day. As he rehearsed his routine, he saw me playing with my coins. He asked, "John, do you want to learn my routine?" What a treat! In fact, almost every day at lunch, we would spend about 20 minutes refining my sleight-of-hand skills. He was so generous with his time and mentorship.

Only now do I realize how special that month was. Doug was a consumate professional.

A few years later, another amazing opportunity arose. Back when I was lighting supervisor at California State University, Northridge (CSUN), my boss had a heart attack, and I was hired to replace him while he recovered . One day, I received a call from a local lighting company called Colortran. They were looking for some students to come work at their factory and learn the ins and outs of their new dimming system called ENR. I recommended my friend, Danny, for the job. We both ended up working at the factory in Burbank for a couple months, learning all about the state of the art dimming system. Danny was quickly hired away by an independent design firm, who designed the diming system, while I continued to work for Colortran.

My boss at Colortran, Gene, asked me if I would like to go to Vegas for a few weeks to supervise the installation of their new dimming system at The Mirage hotel. I love Vegas, so I packed my bags and hopped on the plane. Before I knew it, I was walking through the halls of the hotel prior to its opening.

Vegas was a union town. Not being a union electrician, I was not allowed to touch anything. I would demonstrate the intricacies of installing this high-tech dimming equipment and then disappear for a few hours. After a few days, the hotel electricians decided that it would be OK to let me help as it was a very large job.

We installed dimmers in the showroom which had been designed specifically to host Siegfried and Roy's newest illusion show and in all the hotel meeting rooms. There was even a small 12 dimmer pack installed in Steve Wynn's private office.

During those few weeks, I was introduced to the director of security for The Mirage hotel. He gave me a tour of the hotel's surveillance center. From all of the gambling movies I had watched, I pictured it to be a set of catwalks above the gaming floor. Well, this was far from the case. I walked into this very large narrow room which contained 50 or more floor to ceiling equipment racks filled with video recorders and a console with two chairs and two very large monitors.

Curiosity got the best of me as I asked how many cameras there were. I was told over 1500 and each was connected to one of those video recorders. I asked how was it possible that only two people could monitor all of those 1500 video cameras and catch anyone cheating. He smiled and said "John, the purpose of those video recorders and cameras is not to catch anyone cheating." I'm sure the confused expression on my face prompted him to continue to say, "All of this equipment is here to prove people were cheating."

My next logical question was, "How do you catch people cheating?" He shared with me the fact that at all hours of the day or night, there was a private investigation agency who employed people to sit at tables and gamble. They would look for cheaters.

If they saw something suspicious, they would get up and go to a house phone and dial a special number and report the incident to hotel security. The security personnel would rewind the video recorder for that table and see if cheating occurred. Even the casino, dealers and floormen didn't know these people were spying on everyone. Lesson; If you are gambling in Vegas, and inclined to cheat, beware of your fellow players.

The other interesting fact that I learned was that every slot machine throughout the property was networked. Back then, the slot machines used coins instead of paper tickets. The casino would monitor the weight of the coin reservoirs in the machines.

Vegas gambling regulations state that it is illegal for the casino to manipulate the odds of a slot machine in the casinos favor, but the regulations say nothing about regulating the odds in the players favor. This allowed the casinos to program a slot machine to pay off just a little when those coin reservoirs got close to capacity. This way they were able to prevent the machines from jamming requiring a fleet of casino personnel to be on call to empty the slot machines.

This allowed players to continue playing. Casinos then had a smaller crew empty the machines at 3 o'clock in the morning when the casinos had fewer gamblers. The casinos saved millions of dollars in wages and employee benefits not having to have a huge team on call 24 hours a day. The old adage is very true. The casinos were not built on winners, but losers. They had every aspect figured out.

All of these job experiences, and many more, gave me my skills and understanding of various different types of systems. This allowed me to be knowledgeable in many different areas.

Siegfried & Roy

As graduation at CSUN loomed, I took a leap of faith. My earlier computer experience, from high school and college, prepared me to found my own I.T. support company, JDK Consulting. Soon, I found myself teaching students and faculty alike how to use and network their computers.

My business started out slowly, giving me time to experience some fun, and often unexpected, opportunities.

One of these amazing adventures came when the brother of a close college friend of mine reached out, as he knew that I had computer skills. He worked with Bernie, who managed Siegfried and Roy. This dynamic duo were the hottest magic act in Vegas. Their flamboyant style combined amazing illusions with appearing tigers and other rare and dangerous animals.

Roy had expressed a desire to learn how to use a computer. One thing led to another and I found myself on a flight to Vegas, armed with a brand new, state-of-the-art laptop.

A driver met me at baggage claim, holding a sign displaying my name. I followed him to an awaiting stretch limousine. Now, this was first class treatment, and it only got better. After a short drive, we arrived at Siegfried and Roy's opulent home, which they called their "Jungle Palace." I was escorted into a bungalow just outside of the main house which had been turned into an office. Nervously, I set up the new laptop and waited to meet two of the world's most famous magicians.

A few minutes later, in walked both Siegfried Fischbacher and his partner, Roy Horn. Roy sat at the desk with me as Siegfried sat in a chair across the room. To this day, I remember the expression on Siegfried's face. It was one of disbelief and amusement at the fact that Roy was really going to learn how to use a computer.

As I showed Roy the basics of how to boot the laptop and manipulate the track pad, it became clear this was going to be a challenge. I guided his hand until he learned how to move the cursor around the screen and the difference between a single and double click.

A few minutes later, Roy paused. He said, in his thick German accent, "John, I'm sorry , I don't think this is for me after all." I reminded him that it was his desire to enter the computer age, and to please give me a few more minutes to help him get the hang of it

To his credit, Roy gave it the old college try, but after another 10 minutes, he made me a proposal. If I stopped the lesson and returned the computer, I was welcome to spend the rest of the afternoon enjoying their amazing home. And to top it off, he invited me to be their special guest at their evening show at The Mirage. He assured me that his company would still pay for the computer and my time.

This was a once-in-a-lifetime opportunity. I quickly packed everything up and joined the two for a wonderful lunch inside their 8500 square foot magical mansion. As we ate, they graciously shared many amazing stories from their extraordinary career.

After lunch, I met their head animal trainer. Siegfried and Roy left me in his capable hands. "Ok, here we go," he said. We ventured outside and I received a tour of the property, meeting many of their wild animals that they hand raised and trained for their show. Lions and tigers and bears, oh my!

Picture Licensed through Alamy.com

The tour lasted about and hour and ended with another trainer, who introduced me to an adorable white tiger cub that she cradled in her arms. "Feel free to pet him," she said. The cub was so soft and gentle. She told me that he was born at the Jungle Palace and was Roy's pride and joy. His name was Mantacore. My only regret was that I did not have a camera to record these priceless moments of sheer joy!

Tragically, this was the same white tiger that seriously injured Roy in October of 2003, ending their illustrious careers. When Roy tripped and fell to the ground, Mantacore reportedly grabbed him by the neck and drug him off stage to safety.

I got back in the limousine and the driver casually asked me who I was as he drove me to The Mirage. I said that I was just a guy they hired to try and teach Roy how to use a computer. The driver said that I lucked out because very few people ever recieved this kind of star treatment. I checked into the hotel and took a short nap. About an hour before their 8 pm show, I went to the box to office to get my ticket to the show.

I was met by the show's stage manager. She apologized profusely and told me that evening's show was 100 percent sold out. She knew I was Roy's guest and suggested that I might want to see the show from the lighting booth. "Are you serious?" I shared with her that I was a recent technical theater graduate and I would be honored. I followed her up a set of hallways and stairs and sat in a chair right next to hers.

I had seen the show before so my attention was focused on all that was happening to produce that evenings spectacle. The theater at the Mirage was custom designed for their show. There was a semicircle ramp that went from one side of the stage to the other. The expensive VIP seats were positioned in the area between the front of the stage and the ramp.

At one point in the show, a huge elephant ran along the ramp. Without missing a step, the elephant lifted its tail and dropped a nasty present in the center of the ramp. The stage manager immediately started talking with the backstage crew, arranging a break in the show to clean up the mess. Before we knew it, Roy was running towards the ramp from stage left. We all hoped he would see the obstacle and stop.

Being the consummate performer, he held his head high, looking deep into the audience and continued running . All of us in the booth cringed at what unfolded next. Like in slow motion, he managed to kick it into the VIP seats. We all winced at the sight of spectators being hit in the face by this huge pile of elephant dung.

The stage manager stopped the show as ushers and crew attended to the poor victims. The rest of the audience groaned and screamed, being thankful that it was not them. Keeping his professional composure, Siegfried came to the edge of the stage and raised his hands to quiet the crowd. At this point, the only sound you could hear was from the dozen or so audience members being escorted out of the theater.

In Siegfried's thick German accent, he addressed the crowd, "Ladies and gentlemen, I'm very disappointed in you. Everyone knows , shit happens!" The audience erupted in laughter. After a few minutes, the lights dimmed and the show continued. That was a day I will never forget.

Fast forward 20 years, I was backstage in the Magic Castle Close-up Gallery preparing for my last show of the evening. On cue, Bob, the host, peeked in the side door and asked if I was ready to start. I gave him the A ok. He then said that he had a little surprise for me. I asked what it was. With a wink, Bob replied, "You'll know in just a moment." After he introduced me, I came out through the curtain and took my seat behind the performance table. I looked out into the audience and there sat Siegfried with Princess Irene, the wife of Bill Larsen, the co-founder of the Castle. It was my absolute honor to perform for these two living legends.

At the end of the show, the audience filed out of the theater as Siegfried came to shake my hand and compliment me. I thanked him, and asked if he remembered that young college kid who had come to his home to teach his partner how to use a laptop. "That was you?" he asked. I nodded, yes.

He graciously invited me to join him for dinner. What a magnificent man Siegfried was! As the dream evening drew to a close, he posed for a photograph with me in the lobby.

FIESTA
PARADE FLOATS

I had a lot of friends, who were theater majors. One in particular was a gentleman named Scott. He had been hired as Animation Director for Fiesta Parade Floats. Fiesta was one of the select companies responsible for designing and executing floats for the Tournament of Roses Parade. Scott hired me and a few of his friends to help him build the animation. One day, he told me privately that he was leaving to become the cinematographer on a major movie and he was going to suggest to Fiesta's owners that they hire me to finish the job. After some negotiations, Fiesta and I came to an agreement and now it was my responsibility to not only assemble all of the animation, but make sure everything worked for the parade.

I had no idea what I was getting myself into. In the two weeks before the parade, I worked at least 120 hours a week. Fortunately, school was out for the holidays so I didn't miss too many classes. One of my fondest memories was the first judging of the floats, which took place two or three days before January 1st. The floats were completely surrounded by scaffolding and hundreds of kids, throwing glue, seeds and flowers, which landed on the float, but also in many of the motors and gears that ran the animation. The most complex float was the Eastman Kodak film company dragon whose head moved up, down, and side to side, as it breathed out smoke and fire.

This float had a dozen bowls with rotating flames run by windshield wiper motors, six on each side. We really weren't ready, but scrambled to remove the scaffolding as the judges walked from one float to the next. My biggest concern was that the Kodak float animation would not be working because I had not been able to test it for weeks.

The scaffolding was removed from the Kodak float. I turned on the animation. I saw that the judges were just two floats away. I inspected the Kodak float and noticed that one set of flames were not spinning.

I had no time to get a ladder out and try and resolve the issue. I quickly reached at my belt and removed my walkie-talkie holster. With careful aim, I threw the holster and it hit the flames, causing them to start turning. The holster then fell conveniently into the flame bowl and was out of sight. What a relief. After the first judging, my crew and I were able to go to a local hotel and get a couple hours of sleep before we headed out to test all the animation.

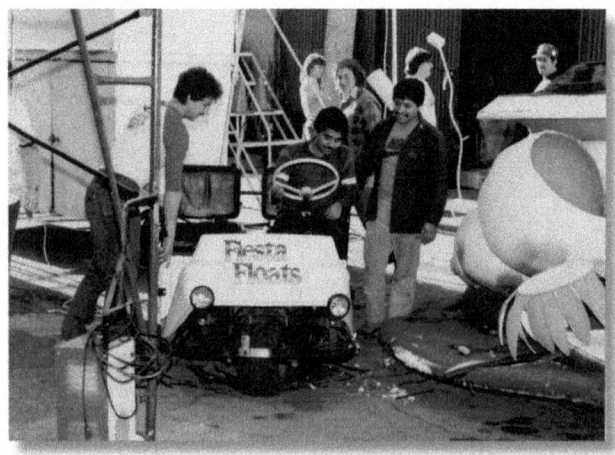

We had at our disposal an electric golf cart which we used to zip around the parade float route.

Pictures Courtesy of Fiesta Floats

The initial plan was for all of Fiesta's floats to be bunched up over one block of the route so that we could test all the animation and communication systems before they were dispersed over the five mile route. Unfortunately, a float from another company broke down on the bridge that all the floats needed to take to get to the parade grounds. It took hours upon hours to get that float towed, so the plan changed. To our dismay, we discovered that when the floats arrived, they would be positioned not in a bunch, as was promised, but along the parade route.

Legends of the Orient   Fiesta Floats

Because we had a lot of downtime waiting for the floats to arrive, we managed to drain the battery on our golf cart. We were then forced to run up and down the five mile parade route testing all of the animation. This is after having worked hundreds of hours in the previous few weeks. Thank goodness I was in good physical shape . That year, eight of our 12 floats won trophies. The owner of Fiesta even gave me a bonus for the excellent work my crew and I did.

JDK
Consulting

After I graduated, I got to work on a few remaining theater projects at CSUN, I worked with a lighting designer, Peggy Dunn on a playwright festival. Peggy and I got to be fast friends. When she learned that I had computer experience, she invited me down to the production company she worked for called Harmony Pictures. Harmony was in the business of producing television commercials. Within an hour or two of arriving, I had solved their computer woes. They immediately hired me as their main I.T. guy.

I started working with the many freelance producers and production managers who were tasked with producing the day-to-day aspects of the commercials. Most of these freelancers were used to doing everything by hand with paper and pen. As luck would have it, Apple released its line of the first powerbook laptop computers. These freelancers ran out and bought this high tech gear, but were at a loss as to how to use it. They started hiring me to set up the machines and show them how to use them .

As my client roster bloomed, My I.T. business now became my main endeavor. It was time for me to focus and stop accepting these odd jobs.

I now had as many as six employees working for me. I had built a very successful consulting firm with offices in Los Angeles and New York. I was making very good money and was having the time of my life.

I was very happy as things were looking up.

PEARLS OF WISDOM
Inner Voice

Taming Your Inner Voice

We all possess an inner dialogue that communicates with us. While this voice can be supportive, it can also turn negative and critical at times. Learning to manage this inner dialogue can significantly enhance our self-perception and overall outlook on life. Here are some straightforward steps to help you gain control over it.

Tune Into Your Inner Voice

The first step is to become aware of what your inner voice is expressing. Is it uplifting or discouraging? Jot down some recurring thoughts to understand what you tell yourself.

Recognize Negative Thoughts

After identifying what your inner voice conveys, look for recurring themes. Do you often think phrases like, "I can't do this" or "I'm not good enough?" Acknowledging these negative thoughts is crucial, as it lays the groundwork for transformation.

Challenge Negative Thoughts

When you catch yourself thinking negatively, question its validity. For instance, if your inner voice claims, "You always fail," reflect on instances where you succeeded. Counter these negative thoughts with factual evidence.

Practice Patience and Self-Compassion

Learning to manage your inner voice requires time. Be patient with yourself as you navigate this journey. Show yourself the same kindness you would offer a friend in need.

Substitute with Positive Affirmations

Formulate positive statements to replace the negative thoughts. For example, transform "I can't" into "I can learn." Recite these positive affirmations to yourself each day. This practice helps retrain your mind for a more positive perspective.

Embrace Mindfulness

Mindfulness involves being fully present and aware of your thoughts without judgment. When negative thoughts surface, acknowledge them but don't allow them to take control. Take deep breaths and concentrate on the present moment to soothe your mind.

Reduce Comparisons

Often, our inner dialogue becomes critical when we measure ourselves against others. Keep in mind that everyone has their own unique journey. Rather than comparing, concentrate on your personal growth and celebrate your distinct qualities.

Cultivate a Positive Environment

The influences around you can shape your inner voice. Surround yourself with supportive friends and family who encourage you. Steer clear of negative settings that fuel your inner critic.

By implementing these strategies, you can learn to control your inner voice. It involves listening to its messages, challenging negative thoughts, and replacing them with positive affirmations. With practice, you can foster a more encouraging inner voice that supports your growth and success.

ACT 5

As Luck Would Have It

"When it comes to luck, you make your own."
- Bruce Springsteen -

I often experience unusual luck. Just after college, I had a particularly memorable incident where I ended up having three cars towed within just four hours.

I was on my way to a client's office on Melrose Avenue for a repair that was expected to take no more than 15 minutes. I arrived around 1:30 PM and parked at a meter directly in front of the entrance. As I dropped a few quarters into the meter, I noticed the parking sign which indicated no parking from 3 PM to 7 PM.

After heading upstairs to meet with the company owner, he showed me the issue, which ended up taking about 20 minutes to fix. Just as I was gathering my things to leave, he asked if I was billing him for an hour since he had a few more tasks he wanted me to handle while I was there. He kept piling on requests, and I lost track of time. Eventually, I had to tell him I needed to leave. When I walked downstairs, I was shocked to find my car had vanished. I returned upstairs to share the unfortunate news with my client, who seemed genuinely remorseful for keeping me longer than anticipated.

Being an early adopter of technology, I had installed Tele-track in my car, enabling me to log into a website to pinpoint my vehicle's exact location. Within five minutes, I discovered my car was towed to a yard about a quarter of a mile away.

Feeling sympathetic and somewhat accountable, my client kindly offered to give me a ride to retrieve my car. We drove past the tow yard, and he dropped me off.

I entered the building and informed the woman at the window that my car had been towed and I was there to reclaim it. She requested my license plate number, which luckily was printed on my insurance card, as I hadn't memorized it. After entering the number into her computer, she apologized, stating, "We don't have your car at this time." Frustrated, I insisted that they did have my vehicle. She maintained that it might still be in the process of being towed. I presented her with the Tele-trac report I had printed out, yet all she could say was, "Sorry, sir. We don't have your car."

Just as she finished speaking, a woman entered and handed her a slip of paper confirming that my car was indeed there. I paid the fee, emptying my wallet of its last $300 and finally retrieved my car. Thankfully, I still had time to reach my final client of the day whose office was only about a mile away.

The office manager and I had developed a friendly rapport, and I had planned to take her out for dinner after I resolved their IT issues. About an hour later, I asked her what she would like for dinner and suggested sushi. She was excited about that idea. One of my favorite sushi spots was a little hidden gem in the valley called Sushi Nozawa. Although Amanda had never been there, I assured her that their fish was exceptional. She proposed following me in her car since I lived in the valley while she resided in Culver City, which was in the opposite direction.

As we arrived at the restaurant, we found the parking lot completely full. Noticing a small shopping center across the street with ample parking, I pulled in, and she parked right next to me. We both got out, walked across the street, and entered the restaurant. Sushi Nozawa did not disappoint. After I paid the bill, we stepped outside, only to discover that both of our cars were missing. That's when I spotted the sign indicating that any vehicles left in the lot after 6 PM would be towed. Seriously?

I managed to stop the last tow truck driver just as he was leaving the lot. Curious about the location of our cars, I asked him where they were, and he informed me they were in Glendale, which was about a 20-minute drive away. I inquired if we could get a ride to retrieve our vehicles, and he begrudgingly agreed. She squeezed in between the sweaty tow truck driver and me. There we were, bouncing around in the cab of the tow truck as we made our way to Glendale. I couldn't help but burst into laughter at the absurdity of having three cars towed in just four hours. I glanced over at her to see that she wasn't sharing in my amusement. I reassured her that I would cover her tow fee and suggested we simply enjoy the ride.

Upon arriving at the tow yard, she dashed inside, and I followed her in to find an ATM. I withdrew $600 to pay the $300 for both tow fees. Without even a word of gratitude, she grabbed her keys and hurried out to her car. I tried to apologize, saying something like, "Just think of the story we'll have to tell; no one will believe it!" She simply said goodbye and got into her car. At that moment, I questioned whether there would ever be a second date—probably not.

Turning to go inside and settle my own tow fee, I watched in disbelief as another tow truck backed into my car. The driver stepped out to assess the damage and I saw that he had managed to crush both passenger side doors. I remarked, "I bet you're glad the owner of that car isn't around." He smiled and nodded. I then introduced myself as the owner, and asked him to follow me inside.

We approached the counter, and asked to speak with the manager. The tow truck driver, the manager, and I went outside to assess the damage. The manager was very kind and stated that all I needed to do was provide two estimates, and they would cover the cost of repairing my car. He also waived the $300 towing fee for my vehicle.

The following week, I obtained three estimates and faxed the two highest ones to the manager. He decided to pay the lower of the two and promptly sent me a check. I chose the most affordable quote, and when everything was settled, I ended up nearly $800 ahead, even after covering dinner and the towing fees.

I enjoy sharing this story because it seems so incredible. Scouts honor, that's exactly how it unfolded.

ACT 6

An Unexpected Twist of Fate

"The world breaks everyone and afterward many are strong at the broken places. But those that will not break it kills."
- Ernest Hemingway -

On Monday, January 7, 2002, I woke up at 7 AM. The previous night, I had been eager to kick off the new year. Despite 2001 being overshadowed by the events of 9/11, it turned out to be a remarkable year for my computer consulting company, JDK Consulting. Following the tragedy, clients sought advanced backup systems, leading to the expansion of my company to six employees and an office manager.

Upon waking, I heard a noise resembling a smoke alarm, ringing loudly in my left ear. Hoping it would subside, the ringing persisted for about 10 minutes. Concerned, I called my dad, who recommended his ENT in Beverly Hills - a respected yet costly specialist who didn't accept insurance. Despite the expense, I sought the best care.

Informing my team of my health issues, I took the day off, instructing them to manage in my absence. I scheduled an appointment with the doctor for 4:30. Unable to go back to sleep, I opted for a walk and ended up having breakfast at a local deli. Watching the news, the ringing in my ear began to diminish, but I proceeded with the doctor's appointment. Arriving in Beverly Hills, I reached the doctor's office around 4.

After completing the new patient paperwork, I was ushered into a waiting room to begin a hearing test. Soon after, the audiologist took me into a soundproof booth for further examination.

I put on headphones at the start of the hearing test. Following the instructions, I raised my hand whenever I heard a tone. The test began with my right ear, playing a sequence of sounds. She then moved on to my left ear, repeating the same process, confirming that both ears passed the test.

Later, the friendly doctor reviewed the hearing test results. As a precaution for a potential ear infection despite no specific cause for the ringing in my ear, he prescribed antibiotics. I left the clinic feeling relieved, hoping for a quick recovery. The next day, I woke up feeling much better.

In my consulting role, I primarily managed phone calls and office tasks while delegating on-site visits to my team. During a conference call with a client, I noticed difficulty hearing men's voices using my left ear. Despite completing the antibiotic course, I initially ignored the issue, hoping it would resolve on its own.

After a couple of weeks, the hearing problem persisted. I contacted the doctor and scheduled another appointment. A few days later, I returned to Beverly Hills for another hearing test. Following the test, the doctor confirmed that I had passed it once again. Despite examining my left ear and finding nothing wrong, he couldn't explain why I struggled to hear men's voices on the phone. Feeling a bit frustrated, I left the office and continued using my right ear for phone calls.

Symptoms Worsen

A month later, I woke up one morning feeling a bit lightheaded and dizzy, a common symptom for me due to allergies. Taking some allergy medication and resting helped alleviate it. With no appointments that day, I did light work and watched TV.

The dizziness subsided after a few hours but returned the next morning, making it hard to focus. Concerned, I visited my family doctor, who conducted a thorough physical exam but couldn't pinpoint the cause. Despite mentioning previous ear ringing issues, he didn't find a connection and advised me to call back in a week if the symptoms persisted.

The dizziness worsened to the point where standing or walking made me feel unsteady and required all my concentration to appear normal. Seeking another opinion due to anxiety, a different doctor conducted a detailed examination and ran blood tests, which all came back negative. Unfortunately, there was still no explanation for the persistent dizziness.

The symptoms persisted, causing me to feel scared and distressed, impacting my overall quality of life. Realizing the need for a brain MRI, I located a new ENT specialist in Encino who was covered by my medical insurance. After scheduling an appointment with the ENT, he recommended a hearing test. Despite having undergone three such tests in the past three months, I agreed to proceed.

His audiologist, a recent graduate, was enthusiastic about identifying the cause of my hearing and dizziness issues. During the hearing test in the soundproof booth, she confirmed my excellent hearing abilities in both ears. Surprisingly, she proposed another test, adding, "John, you aced the hearing tests, but if you have a few more minutes, I'd like to perform another test."

She described it as a hearing decay test. Instructing me to raise my hand when I heard a tone and lower it when the tone faded, she began with my right ear. Raising and lowering my hand accordingly, she then moved to my left ear. After a repeat test, she seemed surprised. She informed me that she was still playing the tone, when I had lowered my hand, leading her to consult her audiology school professor.

Following their discussion, she suspected I might have a rare brain tumor called an Acoustic Neuroma and advised an immediate MRI scan. Although my new ENT assured me about the rarity of Acoustic Neuromas, he still suggested an MRI for confirmation. Being claustrophobic, the idea of an MRI stressed me out further.

During the appointment, I expressed my concerns to the technician. As I lay on the examination table, he instructed me to stay still and assured me that I would still hear his guidance over the loud noises.

My anxiety was escalating as I was moved into the tube during the MRI. Within 30 seconds, panic set in, mostly due to the fear of being unable to sit up. Feeling completely traumatized, I asked the technician to stop and remove me from the tube. I then left and drove home. My stress level peaked. Understanding the importance of the MRI, I was determined to find a solution that would work for me. After reaching out to other nearby centers, I inquired about MRI options for claustrophobic individuals.

A helpful lady at one of the centers presented me with a solution. She explained that their MRI machines were equipped with a periscope-like device, allowing me to see the examination room through mirrors as if I were physically present. She told me that many claustrophobic patients found this setup tolerable. Grateful for the information, I scheduled the test.

A week later, I visited this new center, where the technician detailed the periscope-like view. It helped ease my nerves, and although it was still challenging, I managed to endure the procedure. Little did I know they would have to repeat it. Firstly, without an IV, and then with an IV containing contrast. Post-test, I inquired with the receptionist about obtaining a copy of the films.

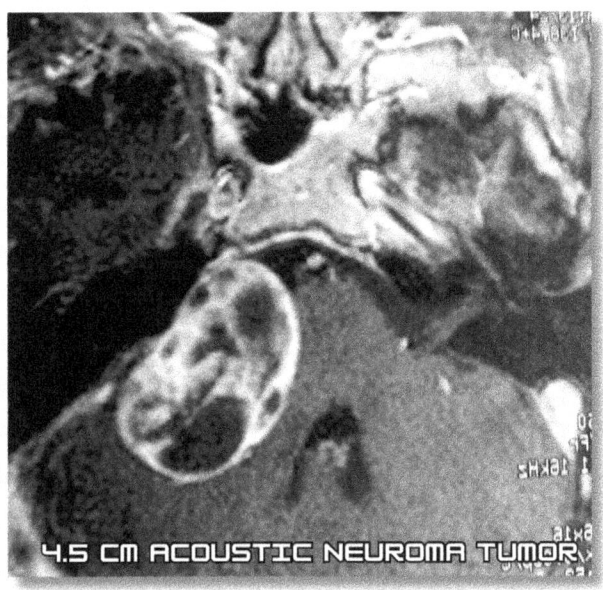

4.5 CM ACOUSTIC NEUROMA TUMOR

She clarified that the initial set would be sent to the radiologist for analysis and then forwarded to my doctor. Persisting, I asked about purchasing the set of films directly, and she disclosed the cost of $300. I handed over three $100 bills, received the films, and made my way to the car.

Diagnosis

I returned to the ENT's office without an appointment, eager to learn about the contents of the films. Taking charge, I approached the reception desk, catching the receptionist's curious glance. Luckily, the doctor was nearby. I quickly informed him that I had my films and asked if he could review them. He escorted me to his office where he examined one of the films on a light board. After a few moments he turned to me with a concerned expression, saying, "John, I see something I don't like." He picked up the phone and scheduled an appointment with an expert Otologist at the House Ear Clinic in downtown LA, for the following day at 11 AM.

He advised me to bring the films along and update him afterwards. While I was taken aback and anxious, his prompt attention and referral to a specialist provided a glimmer of hope for answers to my condition.

Upon arriving home, I promptly phoned my parents to update them on the situation. They offered to accompany me, but I declined, assuring them I would manage on my own. Looking back, this decision proved to be a misstep. With a plan in place, my stress lessened, hopeful that a doctor could finally address my dizziness and hearing troubles.

The following morning, I registered at the front desk, submitting my MRI scans and completing additional paperwork. Before I could finish, my name was called, and I was escorted to an examination room. Anticipation coursed through my veins as I sat on the table, restlessly tearing the tissue paper covering it and swinging my legs back and forth while I waited for the doctor's arrival.

After ten minutes, the specialist entered, studying my MRI scans before making a call to a colleague. Soon after, a neurosurgeon joined the discussion. Observing my scans, they conversed while examining the images. The neurosurgeon exited, and the otologist delivered the shocking news: "Mr. Kippen, you have a 4 1/2 cm Acoustic Neuroma brain tumor. It is displacing your brain stem, leading to your dizziness. In essence, it poses a threat to your life. Surgery is scheduled for next Monday, with a five-day hospital stay expected. You will lose all hearing in your left ear, and there is a possibility of facial weakness post-surgery, which we will strive to minimize." With that, he exited the room.

I went into shock. What did he just say?

He has to do brain surgery?

At that moment, I wished I had brought someone with me as I had numerous questions. Upon opening the door, I heard his voice from an adjacent office. I knocked, the door opened, and there he was seated on a low stool dictating a thank-you note to my ENT for the referral. I informed him that our meeting wasn't over and that I still had questions. He rose, and we returned to the examination room.

I inquired about the necessity of surgery versus radiation as a treatment option. The doctor clarified that such tumors are generally benign, but due to its size, radiation could potentially make it malignant. I then asked about the surgical procedure.

He described, "We make an incision behind your ear, extending past your temple. A small portion of your skull is removed, and the tumor is gradually extracted. Your tumor is intertwined with your acoustic or hearing nerve, balance nerve, and facial nerve. Picture these nerves interwoven like wet linguini pasta. As we remove the tumor, we must be extremely cautious not to damage your facial nerve. After the tumor removal, we create an incision in your abdomen, and extract some belly fat to fill the void left by the tumor removal. The skull piece is then replaced, and you are sutured. Over time, your brain will assimilate the graft and gradually reposition itself post-tumor removal."

The only question that came to mind was if they could take all the fat from my big belly.

This was the first time I witnessed the doctor smiling. He gently said, "Sorry John, that's not our job."

My mind was flooded with questions: How long would the recovery take? Would the surgery be painful? How many days would I spend in the hospital? What other side effects should I expect? Did I really have to lose hearing in my ear?

He had answers to only a few of my questions. Impatiently, he kept looking at his watch, knowing he was late for his next appointment. He scheduled a pre-operative appointment and hearing tests later in the week, advising me to jot down any additional concerns for our next meeting.

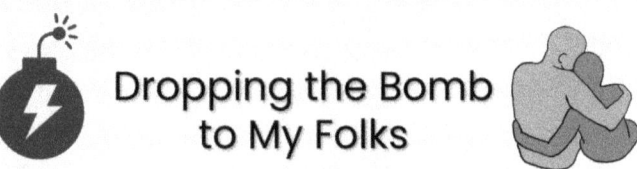

Dropping the Bomb to My Folks

I promptly called my family and we met for lunch at our beloved restaurant, Ca Del Sol. During the 20-minute drive, I tried to stay composed, not wanting to alarm my parents. However, my mind was racing with the doctor's words, which seemed to blur the more I dwelled on them. I wished I had recorded the conversation to recall his diagnosis accurately.

Upon reaching the restaurant, I joined my parents at an outdoor table, where an apprehensive silence lingered. I shared the news that I had a 4 cm Acoustic Neuroma brain tumor to be removed the following Monday, with an estimated 8-hour surgery and a 5-day hospital stay. My parents bombarded me with questions, many of which I couldn't answer. I told them that I would seek clarification during my upcoming appointments. Despite their attempts to console me, the uncertainty of the situation left us all unsettled.

Upon returning home, my first action was to search Acoustic Neuroma on Google. Unfortunately, all I found were distressing stories. The more I delved into my research, the more fearful I became. The doctor's advice about avoiding internet searches now made sense. It appeared that individuals with illnesses tend to share negative experiences online, while those with positive outcomes are less vocal.

With surgery planned in just six days, I needed to address several pending matters. My dedicated employee, Mark Floyd, who had been with me for five years, had given notice of his move to Florida to pursue his dream of becoming a commercial airline pilot. His relocation was scheduled for the following week. I asked if he could postpone his departure to assist me during and after the surgery. Although uncertain about the recovery duration (estimated at 3 to 4 weeks), Mark understood my predicament but needed to discuss it with his spouse and would let me know ASAP.

Meanwhile, I informed some of my key clients about my upcoming absence and assured them of my team's continued support. Shortly thereafter, Mark contacted me with an offer: if I covered the expenses for a hotel or his extended stay in his apartment for the next month, he would remain to help during my recovery. Gratefully, I accepted his offer and agreed to reimburse him accordingly. I had complete confidence in his ability to manage the responsibilities while I recuperated.

On Thursday, I returned to the ear clinic for my pre-op appointment. After a 20-minute wait, my name was called for a hearing test, which puzzled me as I had undergone numerous tests previously and was informed that I would lose all hearing in my left ear post-surgery. I entered the booth, where both ears were meticulously examined.

Following the test, the audiologist became emotional and teary-eyed. When I inquired about her distress, she announced over the intercom, "John, I just tested your left ear, and your hearing was nearly perfect. It saddens me to know you will soon lose all hearing in that ear." I found myself trying to comfort her. How ironic that was.

I went back to the receptionist, saying that I had some follow-up questions for my surgeon. She explained that he was in surgery and would not be available to speak to me. This was frustrating, as he had promised to address all my queries at the appointment's conclusion.

I was advised to arrive at the St. Vincent Medical Center on Sunday evening for blood tests before my 7 AM surgery on Monday. After heading home, I quickly updated my parents on the situation.

I put on a bold front but was actually feeling uneasy about the impending surgery and recovery. No matter how much the doctors assured me that I was in good hands, my fear level was off the charts.

Picture Licensed through Alamy.com

PEARLS OF WISDOM
Dealing with Fear and Anxiety

Anxiety is an emotion we all encounter at various points in our lives. It can evoke feelings of fearfulness or even paralysis. However, fear doesn't have to dictate our actions.

For me, my upcoming surgery was a notable example. In this Act, I will share some straightforward strategies I've developed in order to manage fear.

Understanding Fear

To begin, it's crucial to grasp what fear truly is. Fear is our body's response to threats, serving as a protective mechanism. For instance, if you come across a snake, fear might prompt you to step back to avoid harm. Yet, at times, fear can become overwhelming, preventing us from engaging in activities we desire, such as public speaking or trying a new extreme sport.

Acknowledge Your Fear

The first step in addressing fear is to acknowledge its presence. When you experience fear, try telling yourself, "I am feeling scared." This simple acknowledgment can help you realize that fear is a common human experience. Everyone encounters fear at some stage.

Take Deep Breaths

When fear strikes, your heart may race, and breathing might feel difficult. A simple method to regain calmness is to practice deep breathing. Find a peaceful location, close your eyes, and inhale deeply through your nose. Hold your breath for a few seconds, then exhale slowly through your mouth. Repeat this process a few times. Deep breathing promotes relaxation in your body.

Talk About Your Fear

Discussing your fears can also be beneficial. Share your feelings with someone you trust, such as a friend or family member. They may have experienced similar fears and can provide valuable support. Often, merely voicing your fear can diminish its intensity and make it feel less daunting.

Gradually Confront Your Fears

Facing your fears can be challenging, but approaching them step by step can make the process easier. For instance, if you have a fear of dogs, start by looking at pictures of them. Next, observe dogs from a safe distance in a park. Gradually, you can move closer and even pet a calm dog. This incremental approach helps build your confidence.

Engage in Positive Self-Talk

The messages you send yourself are crucial. Instead of saying, "I can't do this," try rephrasing it to, "I will do my best." Positive self-talk empowers you and reinforces your capabilities. Reflect on your strengths and previous achievements to help dispel fear.

Reach Out for Support if Necessary

At times, fear can feel overwhelming. If your fear is preventing you from enjoying life or engaging in activities you love, consider speaking with a professional, such as a counselor, therapist or Life Coach. They can offer valuable tools and strategies to help you cope with your fear.

———————————•◊——◊•———————————

Fear is a natural part of life, but it doesn't have to dictate our actions. Remember, you are not alone in this journey.

ACT 7

More Complications

"Comebacks after surgery are not at all easy. After a major surgery the difficult part is to conquer the inner demons. It's all in the mind. Only the individual can overcome their fears."
- Rohit Sharma -

The night before my surgery, my mom, dad and I opted for a small celebration at Pacific Dining Car near the hospital, indulging in a luxurious steak dinner for what could be, as far as I knew, my last supper. After dinner, I arrived, had some blood drawn, and was then escorted to a room to rest before the procedure. Sleep was elusive as I tossed and turned, managing only a few hours of rest. At 6 AM, a nurse woke me, signaling that it was time. I quickly changed into a gown as an orderly prepared to transport me to the pre-op area.

Around 6:30 AM, there was a knock at the door, and the orderly inquired if I was ready. With a confirmation, I hopped onto the gurney, and we proceeded to the surgery floor via the elevator. The cold gurney prompted the orderly to cover me with a blanket during our journey. Upon arrival in the pre-op room, a nurse asked if I wanted my head shaved before or after the anesthesia. I opted for "after."

As we made our way to the operating room, an anesthesiologist halted our progress. She revealed that her services were not covered by my insurance and handed me paperwork to sign. In that moment, on the brink of surgery, the request for payment amused me. Familiar with legal matters, I signed the document with a smile, knowing they would never collect a dime, as I was signing under duress.

Upon lying down on the operating table, the IVs were inserted, and the bright overhead lights blinded me. The anesthesiologist then initiated the countdown, "OK John, start counting backwards from 10. Ready?" I replied, "Yes. 10, 9, 8..." and I was out.

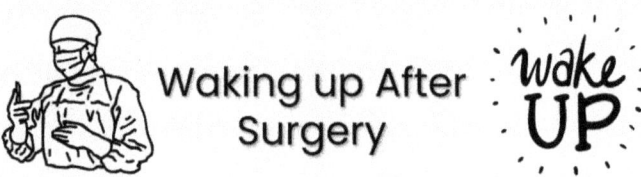

Waking up After Surgery

Upon regaining consciousness, I heard faint voices but found myself unable to respond or move. It felt like being submerged in water, struggling to resurface. After what seemed like hours, but was only minutes, I gradually awoke with a sore neck due to its positioning during the surgery. As my awareness returned, I recognized voices.

Upon requesting my glasses, I gazed at my father's comforting smile. He asked again, "John, how are you feeling?" I responded that my neck was sore, but, other than that I was fine. Little did I know, that was far from the truth. Holding my hand, my father reassured me, "John, everything's gonna be just fine."

I glanced over and spotted my mother standing around six feet away from the bed. I greeted her with a smile, but her expression revealed a sense of horror. Perplexed, I watched as she slowly made her way to the bed. Taking hold of my other hand, she uttered, "John, I'm relieved you're okay," yet her face lacked its usual cheer. Later, I realized it was because the left side of my face had become paralyzed, robbing her of the sight she cherished, her son's smile.

Questions flooded my mind. The only one I recall asking my parents was about the surgery duration. My dad checked his watch and replied, "Fourteen to fifteen hours." Astonishing! I never anticipated the surgery to last that long.

I requested to see the doctors and was informed that my surgeon had left the premises. I inquired if the neurosurgeon could visit me instead. After my parents departed, he arrived to assess my condition. He mentioned that the surgery went smoothly but ran about four hours longer than planned. On a positive note, they successfully extracted the entire tumor.

Before I could voice my concerns, he told me that the facial weakness was likely temporary, as they had closely monitored the electrical activity in my face during the procedure. He explained that the paralysis was probably due to swelling caused by the insertion of my belly fat in my head. Once the swelling diminished, facial movements should return. While emphasizing life's unpredictability, he remained optimistic. Exhausted, I drifted back to sleep, hoping to evade the nickname "Fathead."

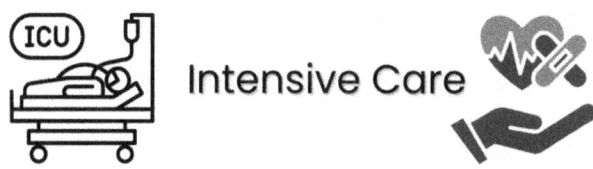

Intensive Care

Upon waking up in the intensive care unit, I found myself surrounded by bustling nurses and connected to numerous wires and tubes, feeling very weak. The nurse had inserted a catheter, minimizing my worry about bathroom visits. Regular check-ins were conducted to monitor any post-surgery complications. Despite my extreme fatigue, I experienced minimal pain, except for neck stiffness. I drifted off to sleep repeatedly, only to be awakened by routine questions and assessments every two hours.

Although I craved rest, the nurse's job required consistent checks, disrupting my sleep. Uncertain if I was dreaming or daydreaming due to lack of rest, these interruptions served as brief escapes.

This pattern persisted, with repeated awakenings hindering my sleep. Inquiring about my ICU stay duration, I was informed it would be a day or two.

Later, an injection was administered to alleviate inflammation. As soon as the needle went into my IV, I felt nauseous and had the urge to vomit. It was a recurring issue every time I received that particular injection, leaving me puzzled. Requesting the nurse to consult the doctor, I couldn't bear the cycle of sickness. Upon the next injection, I vomited once more, still bewildered by my severe reaction. Despite not eating since 8 PM the previous night, the situation persisted. The doctor eventually visited to investigate the cause. I mentioned a possible adverse response to the medication, but the doctor assured me that it shouldn't upset my stomach. However, the symptoms persisted. It suddenly struck me that I had forgotten to disclose my Acid Reflux disease. After receiving an antacid, the problem was resolved.

Another nurse arrived and suggested a bath, although I wasn't keen. Despite my reluctance, she proceeded with a sponge bath, starting with my face, then moving to my chest and arms. The process felt uncomfortable as she inadvertently touched the catheter tube while cleaning my stomach and groin. Each time I winced, she replied, "Oh, it's not that bad." Insisting that she stop, she eventually complied.

My parents visited me in the ICU, lifting my spirits despite my likely disheveled appearance. I greeted them with a smile to ease their concerns. The challenging every two-hour routine persisted for another ten hours until I was finally transferred to a private room.

They brought a gurney and waited for additional help to assist me in moving from the bed. Despite my offer to manage it myself, the nurse chuckled.

After they helped me shift my legs over the edge of the bed, I realized I lacked the strength to even stand. They guided me back onto the gurney and wheeled me to a private room, assuring me that the every two-hour wake-up call was a thing of the past.

The following morning, a physical therapist arrived and explained that I needed to walk around the hospital before being discharged. On my first attempt to rise from the bed, I struggled to even sit upright. He promised to return in a couple of hours. True to his word, he came back and suggested we start by standing with a walker. To my surprise, the dizziness that had plagued me for months had finally disappeared. It was a huge relief. With that, I knew I was on my way to getting back to being normal. I was yet to discover what my new normal would be.

After taking a few steps with the walker, I returned to bed, feeling drained. The therapist told me that he would return the next day, emphasizing the need for effort on my part to hasten my discharge. All I wanted was to leave the hospital.

My good friend Lee Trask

I had a visit from another doctor, this time an eye surgeon, who suggested putting a gold weight in my left eyelid. When I questioned the necessity of the procedure, he observed my eye movements and concluded that we could likely skip the gold weight as long as I kept it lubricated. Having undergone numerous surgeries already, I was relieved by this news. He provided me with a clear eyepatch for nighttime wear and lubricating drops. Interestingly, every time I think or speak about my eye, it starts to water – just like Demi Moore in "Ghost," I can cry on cue.

Shortly after, my dear friends Lee Trask and Romy Sperling visited, showing genuine care and concern. These 2 wonderful women have become two of my closest friends. I deeply appreciate their support and love, both before and after my surgery. My room was soon filled with flowers from my parents, friends, and clients, a heartwarming display of unexpected gifts and cards wishing me well. The day was filled with joy and hope for my recovery, a reminder of the love and kindness surrounding me.

My good friend Romy Sperling

On Thursday morning, determined to break free, I mustered all my strength to rise from bed and slowly navigate the hospital floor. Intercepted by a nurse, she advised me to wait for the physical therapist. Defiantly, I insisted on continuing. However, I only made it halfway before retracing my steps back to bed.

When my parents visited, I updated them on my progress. Their relieved expressions spoke volumes. I grabbed my phone and delved into responding to emails, which boosted my morale and determination to finally get out of this God forsaken place.

In the afternoon, I ventured for a second walk, completing two laps before returning to bed. Relaying my achievement to the nurse, I expressed my readiness to go home, awaiting the doctor's decision.

Friday morning brought the news of my imminent discharge later that day. I requested the removal of the catheter, and upon its extraction, I glimpsed my bandaged head in the mirror for the first time. The sight startled me briefly, prompting a moment of reflection before waiting for my dad to take me home.

By 3 o'clock, my eager father arrived. Despite a delayed discharge process, we maintained composure. Finally, around 4:30, a wheelchair was provided, and after signing release papers and receiving instructions, we headed home. Scheduled for a follow-up at the Ear Clinic on Tuesday, we descended in the elevator and departed.

"The human spirit is more powerful than any drug, and that is what needs to be nourished: with work, play, friendship, family. These are the things that matter. This is what we'd forgotten, the simplest things."
- Robin Williams, Awakenings -

Home Sweet Home

A close family friend, Carmen, had kindly agreed to assist me at home for the week following my surgery. Upon my return, I found that she had already done some grocery shopping and was genuinely pleased to see me. I settled on the couch, focusing on recuperating, and trying to regain a sense of normalcy. I hadn't realized that recovering from brain surgery would necessitate so much rest to feel somewhat like myself again. This led to multiple naps throughout the day.

Around ten in the evening, I went to the bathroom and noticed that the bandages were peeling off. Carefully, I decided to assist them in coming loose. As I turned on the lights and slowly lifted the bandaged beanie cap off my head, I discovered that the adhesive wasn't holding well, possibly due to my greasy hair.

Observing that about six inches of hair had been shaved off, revealing a seven-inch incision from behind my ear to my left eyebrow, which was already showing signs of healing, I opted not to reapply the bandages.

Returning to the couch to watch a movie, I suddenly coughed and felt my neck and T-shirt dampen. Surprisingly, the liquid was clear, not blood. I suddenly remembered that the doctor had warned me about watching for any clear liquid leaking from the incision or my nose, indicating a potential spinal fluid leak. Hoping it would resolve itself, I decided to monitor it until morning. By 8 AM, I noticed moisture at the base of the incision below my ear, signaling yet another complication.

Just when I thought I was safely out of the woods...

I contacted the Ear Clinic and requested to speak with my doctor. The nurse promptly advised me to visit as soon as possible. I phoned my dad, who immediately halted his activities so we could drive back downtown together.

Upon arrival, a nurse mentioned that I needed to undergo a head examination. This was a phrase I had heard loosely many times before. She observed a minor leak near the incision's base and explained that they would re-bandage it with a pressure dressing, hoping for positive results. I was instructed to avoid sudden movements and to lie on my right side as much as possible to aid the healing process.

After returning home with my dad's help, I reclined on the couch, moving cautiously. This time, I left the bandages on, hopeful that they would work. Unfortunately, the following morning, the incision began leaking once more. Following a call to the doctor's office, I was advised to return yet again. They applied another pressure dressing, and I returned home, taking extra care, hoping it would stay secure. Regrettably, a few days later, the incision started leaking again, for a third time.

My dad accompanied me to the examination room this time and insisted on speaking with the doctor. Given that both my parents were attorneys, and my dad specialized in medical malpractice, the doctor's demeanor shifted upon seeing him in the room.

It seemed as if by magic, the doctor's behavior took a positive turn. When my dad inquired about the leak issue, the doctor suggested a solution involving laying on my side and inserting a six-inch needle into my spine to drain the spinal fluid. However, I expressed my reluctance to undergo this procedure and insisted on exploring other options.

The doctor then proposed an alternative of redoing the incision, making a cut in my stomach, removing more belly fat, and repacking the incision, with a shorter hospital stay. The surgery was scheduled for the following day would last approximately two hours. The next morning, my parents drove me to the hospital for the procedure. After being sedated, I woke up in the recovery room feeling more sensitive to the anesthesia.

The new incision in my stomach was painful. The neurosurgeon informed me that he had performed the surgery as my primary doctor was occupied with other matters. This shift in doctors led me to lose trust in my original physician, making me somewhat relieved that the neurosurgeon had taken over.

Around four or five hours later, my parents eventually arrived at my room. Boy, was my dad pissed! Despite the surgery lasting just over an hour, the nurses failed to inform my parents that the procedure was completed. Whenever my dad inquired about my condition, the nurse mistakenly mentioned that I was still in surgery, rather than in surgical recovery. Understandably, this did not sit well with them.

On the way back home, I requested a stop at In & Out Burger to grab some comfort food. A Double Double Burger with cheese and onions, fries, and a chocolate shake really hit the spot. When I settled onto my couch at home, a sense of relief washed over me as I could finally begin the healing process.

The doctor scheduled a follow-up at the Ear Clinic in two weeks. Within a couple of days, I tentatively resumed work on my computer, reaching out to clients and trying to establish a sense of normalcy. However, any exertion left me completely drained, leading to several naps throughout the day. Despite feeling fatigued, I could sense my strength returning.

The most significant improvement was that my dizziness had vanished. The only discomforts were the stitches on my stomach and a staple near the base of my incision below my left ear.

A few days before the follow-up appointment, I decided to remove the bandages to inspect the wound. The staples resembled something out of a *Frankenstein* movie: half an inch long and an inch wide, running from the base of my skull to my temple.

During the follow-up, my doctor promptly greeted me in an examination room. His first question was, "Where's your dad?" I explained that my dad was at work, and I drove myself to the hospital. Surprised, he exclaimed, "You drove? I don't want to hear that." After examining the incision and removing the staples, he advised me to keep it dry and avoid showering for another two weeks. I agreed and drove back home.

Over the following month, my body gradually recovered. While I still needed occasional naps, I felt better overall. As I eased back into work, I sometimes forgot about the paralysis on the left side of my face. It only became apparent when I struggled to drink from a soda can, resulting in spills on my shirt. Straws became my newfound necessity.

This was only the first of many post surgery surprises...

"There is something in the human spirit that will survive and prevail, there is a tiny and brilliant light burning in the heart of man that will not go out no matter how dark the world becomes."
- Leo Tolstoy -

ACT 8

Post Surgery Surprises

*"Hope sees the invisible, feels the intangible,
and achieves the impossible."*
- Helen Keller -

One of the unexpected side effects of my surgery was the loss of hearing in my left ear. The doctor never prepared me for the experience of hearing from just one side. I found myself unable to determine the direction of sounds. In crowded settings, when someone would call my name, I would spin around like a top, desperately trying to make eye contact with the person speaking to me. This was incredibly frustrating and heightened my anxiety about being in large groups.

Another source of frustration in my life is when the battery in one of my smoke detectors starts to run low and begins to chirp. For some reason, this always seems to happen in the late evening.

I have three smoke detectors in my home. I walk to the one in the back room and stand beneath it, waiting for the next chirp. Chirp! I tell myself it might not be this one, so I move to the next smoke detector and wait again. Chirp! Perhaps it's not that one either, so I proceed to the third and final detector and wait. Chirp! As my frustration mounts, with no clue which one needs the battery replaced, I end up calling Gary Cervenka, one of my closest friends, to ask if he can please come over and identify the offending smoke detector, so I can change the battery and finally get some much-needed sleep.

My friend Gary has bailed me out of more jams than I care to admit.

My good friend Gary Cervenka

I have always embraced new technology and was thrilled to discover a feature on my phone called Find My iPhone. One afternoon, I misplaced my phone somewhere in the house. I attempted to call it from my landline, only to realize it was set to vibrate. This was the perfect chance to test out that new feature. I sent a command to my iPhone to produce an alert tone. Who was I kidding?

Without the ability to pinpoint the sound's direction, Gary once again came to my aid. For those with friends and loved ones who are deaf in one ear, please exercise patience, as filtering out background noises can make conversations in loud settings quite challenging.

Oh, and by the way, I've also lost the ability to enjoy music in stereo, making my 7.1 surround sound in my home theater totally useless.

Realizing my New Normal

I had few mirrors at home, and the ones I did have, I tended to avoid. They served as constant reminders of my facial paralysis. A major obstacle I encountered was enunciating words with a double "P" syllable, such as "pepper." Whenever I attempted to pronounce them, my left cheek would release air, distorting that syllable. The irony was in the fact that the double "P" is present in my own last name: Kippen. Life can be strangely unkind.

Upon the doctor's recommendation, I consulted a speech therapist who advised me to slow down and focus on the syllables when pronouncing my last name to improve clarity. After months of practice, this technique became second nature, and I always paused before saying "Kippen."

As my hair regrew, it concealed the incision, except for my bald spot. I gradually resumed going out, only to become depressed by people's prolonged gazes, due to my altered appearance. While adults would briefly glance at my face and then look away, children, being naturally inquisitive, would stare and question my facial paralysis. I lost count of the times a child would observe my face and whisper to their parent, "Mom, what's wrong with his face?" Hoping that my face would recover in about six months, I tried not to let it affect me, trusting the doctors' assurance that the paralysis was temporary.

A few weeks later, I made a house call to a client in Santa Monica. As I was talking to one of the people who worked there, they commented, "John, I think I just saw your face move." That was the best news I'd heard in months. I said "Really, really? Please excuse me." I ran to the bathroom and stood in front of the mirror, trying to smile.

At one point it even looked to me that my face was starting to respond. I was elated! Alas, my excitement was short-lived. After a day or two I realized that what I actually saw was a little jiggle being caused by me being super animated while trying to smile. Another blow to my self-confidence.

3 MONTHS
Hope starting to Fade

I returned for my three-month check-up and waited nearly an hour to be seen. When my otologist finally entered the examination room, he immediately inquired about my dad's well-being before I could speak. I politely redirected the conversation to focus on myself. My main concern was when my facial movement would return. The otologist reassured me that the nerve was only traumatized, not severed, and expected it to recover soon. Satisfied with his explanation and pleased with the healing progress of the incision, I scheduled another appointment for the six-month mark.

As the appointment approached, the Ear Clinic requested a current MRI to confirm the absence of the tumor. I called the imaging center and asked if they still had that periscope MRI machine. They said no. After some searching, I found an MRI center who offered IV sedation, with a doctor's prescription. Relieved, I booked an appointment for the following week.

My friend Gary drove me to the appointment. Once prepped, an anesthesiologist came by and said, "OK John, we're gonna knock you out using Propofol." He explained this was a very quick acting anesthesia, and that as soon as they removed the mask from my face, I would wake up almost instantly, with no lasting effects. As an aside, yes this was the same innocent anesthetic that Michael Jackson abused, which led to his death. I woke up to what seemed just like five minutes later, thanked him, and we drove home.

The following week, I made my familiar trek to the ear clinic. Once again, my first question to the doctor was about when my face would regain movement. His casual reply was that he didn't know and suggested another surgical option: redirecting a nerve from the tongue to the facial nerve. He explained that with time, I would relearn how to smile by clenching my teeth.

Due to my profession involving client interactions, I requested to speak with a few patients who had undergone the experimental procedure. The doctor's nurse provided me with a list of contacts to reach out to. After contacting a few of these patients, most reported improvement in their facial paralysis, but I could detect notable speech impediments which discouraged me from proceeding with this surgery.

With no solution in sight for restoring my smile, my despair grew, leading me to avoid social gatherings and dodge photo opportunities. The flatness of photographs only emphasized the droopiness on the left side of my face, intensifying my self-consciousness.

Social events passed by without my attendance. I opted out of high school reunions and holiday gatherings, as I didn't want those who knew me pre-surgery to witness my transformation. My routine shifted to working from home and occasionally dining out at nearby restaurants.

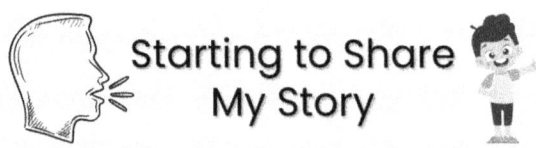

Starting to Share My Story

One evening I went to Tony Roma's for dinner by myself. In the booth behind me was a family of a mom, dad and a little boy. The little boy climbed up on the seat and turned around and started staring at me. This would happen from time to time so I just ignored him.

But this little boy climbed down and came over to me and said, "Mister, what's wrong with your face?" My dry sense of humor tempted me to say, "Well sonny, when I was your age I wanted to be an honest politician so I could talk out of just one side of my mouth." Before I had a chance to respond, his mom grabbed him by the arm, pulled him back and said, "Don't bother the nice man. He has enough troubles already."

Realizing that this could be a great teaching moment, I stood up and approached their table, bending down on one knee. Looking in the child's eyes, I said, "That's a really good question. You see, I had a medical procedure that prevents me from moving my face. But it's my new face and you know what? I love it. I think it's cool because it's different, different like yours." The boy smiled with no judgments. He was only curious. He immediately accepted my explanation, shrugged his shoulders, and said, "Thanks, mister." I looked up at his mom and she was starting to cry. I tried to comfort her by saying, "Oh, don't worry. It happens all the time." I think she realized at that moment that she was imposing her views on her little boy, keeping him from simply being curious.

You know, they often say curiosity killed the cat. Well, my new face sure made room for some interesting conversations. I started to get a pretty thick skin, but every once in a while, someone's hurtful comments would slice through that hard exterior like a hot knife through butter.

"The world accommodates you for fitting in, but only rewards you for standing out."
- Matshona Dhliwayo -

Finding Serenity

It was time for my eighteen-month follow-up appointment. My usual doctor was unavailable, so I saw one of his colleagues, whom I had heard of, but never met. As he reviewed my medical records, I posed the same question, "When will my face start moving again?" Unfamiliar with my case, he inquired about the time since my surgery. I mentioned it had been around eighteen months. Surprised, he asked, "Why did you wait so long?" This caught me off guard. "What do you mean, why did I wait so long?" I had seen my doctor monthly for the first six months, then every six months thereafter until today, asking the same question at each visit. His expression changed, and all he could manage was, an "Oh, I'm so sorry."

He went on to explain that after about a year, the connection points between the nerves and muscles weaken. Even if the nerves were to regenerate, they would not be able to activate the muscles again. I was furious. "Why am I only hearing this now?" His response was apologetic, offering suggestions for plastic surgery. He mentioned that options like a cross facial nerve graft were no longer viable. I should have taken legal action against my doctor, but for some reason, I chose to focus on recovery instead.

Who knows? Maybe I could land a role as The Phantom of the Opera.

> *"You either get bitter or you get better. It's that simple. You either take what has been dealt to you and allow it to make you a better person, or you allow it to tear you down. The choice does not belong to fate, it belongs to you"*
> - Josh Shipp -

PEARLS OF WISDOM
Out of the Box Thinking

Introduction

Thinking outside the box involves generating innovative ideas and solutions that diverge from conventional thinking. It encourages creativity and an open mind. In this section, we will examine strategies to cultivate this type of thinking.

Foster Curiosity

Curiosity is the innate desire to learn and discover more. To think outside the box, begin by posing questions. Avoid taking things at face value; instead, inquire "why" and "how." For instance, when faced with a problem, contemplate its origin and consider alternative solutions. The more questions you raise, the greater your understanding will become.

Alter Your Environment

Your surroundings can significantly influence your thought processes. If you consistently work in the same location, you may find yourself trapped in repetitive ideas. Experiment with different settings; visit a park, a café, or a library. Fresh environments can stimulate new thoughts. You may observe elements you have not noticed before, igniting your creativity.

Engage with Diverse Individuals

Interacting with a variety of people can provide fresh perspectives. Each person brings unique experiences and insights. Participate in clubs, attend workshops, or simply initiate conversations with strangers. Listen to their stories and viewpoints; this can broaden your outlook and inspire new ways of thinking.

Cultivate Creativity

Creativity is a skill that can be honed through practice. Engage in activities that foster creative thinking, such as drawing, writing, or making music. Additionally, solve puzzles or play strategy-based games to enhance your ability to think differently.

Question Your Assumptions

We often hold beliefs that can confine our thinking, known as assumptions. To expand your mindset, actively challenge these assumptions. For instance, if you think there's only one method to accomplish a task, consider whether alternative approaches exist. Strive to break free from these constraints and explore new opportunities.

Take Breaks

Often, the most brilliant ideas emerge when you're not consciously trying to generate them. Allow your mind to rest by taking breaks. Go for a stroll, meditate, or engage in a leisure activity. Stepping away from a challenge can enable your brain to form new connections and discover solutions.

Maintain a Journal

Documenting your thoughts and ideas can enhance clarity in your thinking. Keep a journal to record your questions, insights, and observations. Regularly review it to track how your perspectives evolve over time. This practice can help you identify patterns and spark new ideas.

Cultivating an innovative mindset requires both practice and patience. With dedication and time, you can enhance your creativity and evolve into a more inventive thinker. Opportunities are waiting for you to explore!

Creative Thinking Exercise

I've learned that creative problem solving is a skill that requires practice. Here is a fun puzzle that will help you in thinking outside the box!

I present you with three equal rows, each containing three dots. Your mission, if you choose to accept it, is to connect all the dots by drawing four straight lines without lifting your pencil from the paper. Begin from any dot, but the key is to keep the pencil in contact with the surface at all times. Where one line ends, the next line can begin. Additionally, you cannot retrace any line you have already drawn.

ACT 9

A Welcomed Distraction

" Poker is a fascinating, wonderful, intricate adventure on the high seas of human nature."
- David A. Daniel -

After I began stepping out of my comfort zone, I felt a desire for something new and exciting.

Poker became a hobby for me. I often played with my parents since my dad taught me the game. Becoming a skilled player, I decided to try my luck at the Commerce Casino, playing $3/$6 limit Texas Hold'em. For those unfamiliar with poker, the numbers indicate the betting limits. This was during the era before no-limit poker gained popularity. I sat at the table with $100 in blue chips, each valued at $1.00. In my first hand, I received two red 7s, a decent starting hand, so I called the pot.

The first three community cards, known as the "flop," were the 7 of spades, the 8 of spades, and the 9 of spades, giving me three of a kind, a strong hand but not the best possible hand known as, "the nuts." Another player bet, and I called. The fourth community card, the "turn," revealed the 2 of hearts, not changing the situation much. The other player bet, and I called again. The final card, the "river," was the 7 of Clubs, giving me four of a kind, an excellent hand. My opponent bet, I raised, and he re-raised. I raised once more. As there were only two of us in the pot, we could continue raising until one of us folded, raised again, or just called. Observing the board with the community cards, I noticed three possible straight flushes. I said, "If you have a straight flush, you win. I call your raise."

He then revealed the 10 and Jack of spades, having achieved a straight flush, one of the best possible hands. Disheartened, I lost the pot, roughly $120, but every player experiences bad beats.

Suddenly, the table erupted in celebration, with players congratulating me. Perplexed, a player beside me explained the bad beat jackpot rule. If a player loses with four of a kind or better, and both players use both hole cards to form their hand, the loser receives 60% of a progressive jackpot, the winner gets 20%, and the remaining 20% is shared among the remaining players at the table. I started to feel hopeful but had no clue about my winnings.

A regular player glanced at his watch, turning pale, and mentioned it was a few minutes before 6pm on a Monday. This detail seemed insignificant until he clarified that the Commerce Casino had a special jackpot from 5 to 6 pm on Mondays, totaling $100,000. I had just won $60,000 on my very first live poker hand! After taxes, I managed to make a down payment on my first new car and saved the rest. That money sustained my gambling habit for nearly a decade, letting me play with the casino's funds. I made a promise that once the money ran out, I would limit my gambling activities.

I discovered Hollywood Park Casino in Inglewood, California, closer to where my IT clients were based. It was situated within the renowned race track. To escape rush hour on the north 405 Freeway, I would drive in the opposite direction for about 10 minutes to reach the casino. Following my brain surgery and facial paralysis, I felt restless staying at home. Since I was anonymous there, I would wear a knit cap to conceal my scar and just enjoy playing cards. Surprisingly, the other players paid no attention to my paralyzed face; they were only interested in winning. Despite making only a few friends, one memorable evening, I found myself seated next to a familiar face at a $3/$6 limit Texas Hold'em table.

To my surprise, it was Don Adams, best known as Agent 86 from the '70's TV series "*Get Smart*." Though older and grayer, he was easily recognizable. Accompanied by his caregiver, Don didn't engage much in conversation. During a hand where it was just the two of us, I had two pair while he had four to a straight. Although the "river" card slightly improved his hand, giving him top pair, he missed his intended straight by one card. Unable to resist, I humorously quipped in my best Maxwell Smart voice, "So Don, it looks like you missed it by that much!" This catchphrase was a favorite of his character on the show. Don couldn't help but chuckle at my impression, and from that moment, we became close friends, enjoying many games together until his passing a few years later.

In my comfort zone at the "Jason Alexander Charity Poker Tournament."

One other memorable player I had the privilege of playing alongside was Bill Gates. Every January, during the Consumer Electronics Show in Las Vegas, I would engage in low-stakes poker at the Mirage Hotel. On one occasion, a seat became available, and Bill joined the game, setting a rule that no technology-related questions were allowed. It was a privilege to compete against him and walk away with his winnings. Even though he wasn't particularly skilled at poker, he had a genuine passion for the game.

After six grueling hours, I was proud, and a
bit relieved, to place third.

I also played for enjoyment and always within my limits. I found delight in the psychological aspect of the game, deducing my opponent's hand and influencing their decisions through my betting strategies. This strategic thinking later proved invaluable as I ventured into my magic career.

ACT 10

Magic Rediscovered

" Magic is believing in yourself. If you can make that happen, you can make anything happen."
- Goethe -

Performing magic became my secret weapon after a devastating twist of fate. Picture this: post-surgery for a brain tumor left me with a frozen face, sending me spiraling into a pit of despair. But the real painful moment? Watching my mom's eyes betray her heartbreak as she tried to stay strong.

I had clung to the hope that my facial nerve would snap out of its stupor, as promised by the doctors. Alas, on that dreaded 18th-month checkup, reality hit: my poker face was here to stay.

Switching to remote work to keep afloat, I became a recluse, dodging parties and shrinking my social circle. The outside world became a judgment zone, making dating a no-go and kids' giggles a stab at my heart. The struggle of being a hermit when I used to be the life of the party? Real despair, folks.

Some years later, seeking new interests, I decided to rekindle my childhood passion for Close-up magic. During this time, I was re-introduced to the renowned Magic Castle in Hollywood, California. This 60 year old landmark was an exclusive private club, internationally recognized as "The Carnegie Hall of Magic."

As a non-magician member, I eagerly visited the Magic Castle every Saturday, immersing myself in the captivating performances of world renowned magicians. Witnessing their dedication to the craft inspired me, reigniting a desire to perform again.

With excitement and great anticipation, I auditioned to become a performing member, and successfully secured my gold pin. Now welcomed as a member of this prestigious club, I began entertaining guests with an illusion or two during my weekend visits.

Almost every time I passed through the magic bookcase entrance, I saw a magician named Phil. He also noticed me, lurking in the corners and shadows. Phil opened his heart and graciously extended an invitation to me to join him during any of his performances. His gesture of support allowed me to showcase my talents without the pressure of a full routine, empowering me to present my best effects.

Holding court at my favorite spot in The Magic Castle

Picture by Hocus Pocus Focus - Magic Castle Photographer

Phil's mentorship and belief in my potential were instrumental in boosting my confidence and shaping me into the magician I aspired to become. He saw promise in me, even before I saw it myself, and for that, I tip my hat to him in this magical tale of growth, recovery and wonder.

Within the next few months, I had gathered enough material to confidently present a 20-minute act. Phil and I would alternate performing at a table just outside the renowned Parlor of Prestidigitation.

Shortly after, Phil approached me with a valuable piece of advice. He commended my creativity in magic but noted that my effects predominantly centered around myself. He suggested shifting the focus onto the spectator.

Without delay, I restructured my performances to highlight the spectator as the star, with myself serving as the narrator. This shift marked the inception of the true John the Magician.

Performing a Private Show in the Jack Oakie Gallery

Picture by Hocus Pocus Focus - Magic Castle Photographer

The effectiveness of my magic performances significantly improved as I tailored each act to the spectators' words, actions, and thoughts. This, in turn, resulted in heightened reactions from the audience. Notably, as I began recalling their names and crafting magical moments, I observed a growing sense of engagement among my audiences.

Gradually, regular patrons at the Castle started encouraging their guests to witness my performances, further enhancing my visibility. Post shows, attendees often requested to capture moments with me in the lobby. Although appreciative of their requests and promising a potential meeting later, my unease with photography persisted.

My skills improved to the extent that Joan Lawton, Chairman of the Board of Trustees, would invite me to perform whenever she hosted members of the Armed Forces.

Performing for this fine group of Marines was my absolute honor.

You can tell by the smiles on their faces that they were having the time of their lives.

Pictures by Taylor Wong - Magic Castle Photographer

Always my pleasure to entertain members of the Armed Forces

Performing my original Phoenix Rising Illusion

Pictures by Taylor Wong- Magic Castle Photographer

Magic Live - Healing

To dive deeper into the world of magic, I ventured to my first magic convention, Magic Live, situated in the enchanting city of Las Vegas, in August 2017. Surrounded by legendary magicians and industry stars, I was bursting with excitement to rub shoulders with these magical icons.

On the very first night of the convention, I crossed paths with the esteemed magician, Jeff McBride in a corridor. Pushing past my nerves, I bravely walked up to him and persuaded a kind stranger to snap a picture of us, freezing that magical moment in time.

So, picture this: I met a bunch of legendary magicians and every time I suggested a selfie, they were all up for it! Not a single hint of rejection!

With Grandmaster Magician Jeff McBride

Back home, scrolling through those magical selfies, it hit me, if these wizards had no qualms about posing with my quirky face, why should I? And just like that, the magic of self-acceptance worked its spell! I realized my unique face didn't have to be my whole story.

Armed with newfound confidence, I returned to The Castle, ready to dazzle. I conjured up magic that was close to my heart, and suddenly, I wasn't just mystifying, I was captivating. People were drawn to the real me, shining through my routines.

After 15 years, and thousands of shows, joy made a grand entrance back into my life. Performing became my daily dose of delight, spending countless nights at The Castle, weaving tales with my "magic wand." Show after show, my act was honed to perfection; my hands moving like second nature, allowing me to connect deeply with my audiences.

Magic wasn't just a show, it was my ultimate therapy. It helped me see my facial differences in a whole new light.

It was a joy to meet and spend time with two of the greatest living magicians.

The always amazing Penn & Teller!

"The purpose of art is to collide the intelectual and visceral together at the highest speed possible."
Penn Jillette

ACT 11

A Final Conundrum

*" The face is the mirror of the mind, and
eyes without speaking confess the secrets
of the heart."*
- St. Jerome -

A couple years later, I saw a television special featuring a highly respected Los Angeles based plastic surgeon, renowned for his exceptional work with patients recovering from tragic accidents. Intrigued, I found the doctor's contact information, called him, and scheduled an appointment. Although I had to wait nearly three months, I thought, what was another few months at this stage?

When the day of the appointment arrived, I met the plastic surgeon, a tall, slender man with dark hair who seemed very focused on his work. He examined my face and asked several questions. He mentioned that he had performed numerous surgeries on patients diagnosed with acoustic neuromas, which often led to facial paralysis. This was his specialty.

He presented me with a couple of options, one of which was an extensive surgery involving the removal of a muscle and nerve from one of my legs. They would then sew that muscle into my upper lip and allow the nerve to grow. After a few months, they would reconnect the nerve to the muscle and, following several months of physical therapy, my brain would learn to raise the left side of my face to achieve symmetry with the right. This option seemed very complex and costly.

The next best alternative was a facelift, which would create symmetry at rest. This way, people wouldn't be able to tell I had facial paralysis, and I would gain a new smile that was uniquely mine. This procedure was much simpler, less invasive, and more affordable. I thanked him and said I would think it over as I left.

Picture by Ryan Palmieri

I reached out to my friends and family for their opinions. The consensus was clear: "Oh John, we love your face and your smile. The choice is yours; don't do it for anyone but yourself." After a lot of soul-searching, I ultimately decided to proceed. I called the nurse to let her know I was ready for the facelift procedure. She sent me some forms to sign and assured me she would follow up with a date.

A few days later, she called with exciting news: she had managed to find a date and could fit me in. I replied, "I'm sorry, fit me in?" She confirmed, "Yes, your surgery is scheduled for 4 PM next Friday." I expressed my hesitation about undergoing surgery so late in the afternoon on a Friday. There was a pause on the line, and she replied, "John, I don't understand. I moved mountains to secure that time for you." I responded, "Please do me a favor and move the mountains back."

She perceived me as ungrateful, but all I could think about was not wanting to have surgery at the end of a long week just before a three-day weekend. I preferred to be the Monday morning 7 AM patient.

Ultimately, I decided against the surgery. A couple years went by, and life continued. While I began to embrace life once more, my newfound passion for magic became a source of therapy, allowing me to truly enjoy living again.

As a computer consultant in Los Angeles, I've had the privilege of working with several celebrities over the years. One of them was Jamie Lee Curtis. From our very first meeting, we connected well. After a few years, we transitioned from being mere business associates to becoming close friends. During one of our sessions addressing a computer issue, our conversation took a personal turn. The topic of my face came up, and Jamie, with her strong maternal instincts, sensed my inner struggle. It was clear to her that I was still dissatisfied with the left side of my face and was contemplating surgery.

Jamie Lee Curtis on the set of my documentary

Picture Courtesy of Ryan Palmieri

I shared my experience from my initial visit with the plastic surgeon, realizing that I shouldn't let the insensitivity of his scheduling nurse dictate my decision. Jamie offered to accompany me to see him, which deeply touched me. It was such a thoughtful gesture. I quickly accepted and arranged an appointment that suited her schedule. When we arrived at the doctor's office, we caught the attention of others in the waiting room. Approaching the receptionist, I stated that I was there to see the surgeon, and to my surprise, the usual 30-minute to an hour wait vanished.

We were promptly taken to an examination room, and the doctor came in within just a few minutes. His first question was why I had not gone through with the surgery a couple of years prior. I explained my experience with the scheduling nurse, and he understood my hesitation. He briefly outlined the options for Jamie's benefit, and I sought her opinion. She replied, "John, it's your choice; I support you no matter what." After a few moments, I decided to proceed with the facelift. As our conversation wrapped up, I had one final question.

"Doctor, my final request is for you to bandage my face as it will be done when I leave the surgery center." I explained that I suffer from claustrophobia and wanted to avoid any surprises that could lead to me to accidentally removing the bandages too soon. He replied that this was not something he could accommodate. I clarified that I wasn't asking him to do it personally, but rather for one of his staff to apply the bandages so I could understand what it would feel like, to ensure I could handle it. He expressed doubts about its feasibility. I responded, "Okay, thank you. Jamie, let's go."

In the following years, I realized that I needed to accept my face as it was rather than trying to change it. I began visiting The Castle more frequently, as that's where I felt secure. As I gradually became more comfortable in my own skin, I honed my performance skills and exuded confidence.

PEARLS OF WISDOM
Building Self Confidence

Self-confidence is the belief in your own abilities and intrinsic worth. It involves feeling good about yourself and having faith that you can tackle challenges. While building self-confidence requires time and effort, it is entirely achievable! In this section, we will explore straightforward methods to enhance your self-confidence.

Know Yourself

The initial step in fostering self-confidence is gaining a deeper understanding of who you are. Reflect on your strengths and talents. What skills do you possess? Perhaps you excel as a listener, possess artistic talents, or are a loyal friend. Jot these down. Acknowledging your strengths allows you to appreciate your value.

Establish Small Goals

Setting small, attainable goals can significantly boost your confidence. Begin with simple tasks, such as starting a book, trying out a new recipe, or solving a puzzle. Celebrate your achievements when you accomplish these goals! Each small victory enhances your confidence for tackling larger challenges.

Engage in Positive Self-Talk

The inner dialogue you have with yourself is crucial. Negative self-talk can undermine your confidence. Rather than thinking, "I can't do this," try reframing it to, "I will give it my best effort." Positive self-talk motivates you and reinforces your belief in yourself. Create a list of affirmations, such as "I am capable," and read them to yourself daily.

Embrace Mistakes

Making mistakes is a universal experience, and that's perfectly fine! Instead of feeling disheartened by errors, view them as opportunities for growth. Ask yourself, "What can I do differently next time?" This perspective fosters personal development and strengthens your confidence in your abilities.

Surround Yourself with Support

The individuals you associate with can significantly impact your self-confidence. Spend time with friends and family who uplift and inspire you. Steer clear of those who bring negativity or make you feel inadequate. A strong support network can enhance your confidence and help you feel appreciated.

Step Out of Your Comfort Zone

Venturing into new experiences can be daunting, yet it's an excellent way to enhance self-confidence. Start with small steps outside your comfort zone. This could involve speaking up in class, joining a new club, or exploring a new hobby. Each time you challenge yourself, you grow and build your confidence.

Take Care of Yourself

Prioritizing your physical well-being can also elevate your self-confidence. Focus on eating nutritious foods, exercising regularly, and ensuring you get sufficient rest. When you feel physically well, it can enhance your mood and self-esteem. Dedicate time to activities that bring you joy, such as reading, drawing, or enjoying moments with loved ones.

Dress for Success

The way you dress can significantly influence your self-perception. Wearing outfits that make you feel great can elevate your confidence. Select clothing that showcases your personality while ensuring comfort. When you look your best, you often exude more confidence as well.

Building self-confidence is a journey that requires time and dedication. Remember, everyone experiences moments of doubt, but with each step forward, you can strengthen your confidence and trust in yourself. Keep pushing ahead, and soon you'll be amazed at how far you can go!

"Each life is unique and each journey is different. There is no universal scale for success or happiness. Let's wish one another peace, joy and love, rather than letting jealousy stain our relationships and perceptions. It is time to embrace the beauty of our individual lives, with all their imperfections, challenges and moments of triumph."
- Alphonse Rebmann -

ACT 12

Henry, My Conjuring Companion

"Every Superhero needs a sidekick."
- Anonymous -

What captivated me about my time at The Magic Castle was the ability to alter perceptions. I could proactively address why my face was paralyzed during my magic performances, before anyone inquired. Once people grasped the reason behind it, it transformed into my ultimate superpower.

One evening, while dining at the main bar with my back turned, a guest entered and told the host, "Last time we were here, we saw a fantastic magician, I can't recall his name, but you know him, he's the one with the paralyzed face." Overhearing the conversation, I realized I didn't want to be recognized solely for that.

I took out my phone and searched online, stumbling upon a company in Las Vegas producing pocket squares with built-in lights. Since I often wore a royal blue jacket, I opted for a blue one to match.

Miraculously, this simple change shifted the narrative. I was no longer labeled as "The guy with the paralyzed face," but known as "The magician with the illuminated pocket square." It was astonishing how those familiar with me at The Castle would now direct others seeking close-up magic to look for the person with the blue pocket square. Such a minor adjustment made a significant impact, merely by altering the perspective.

A few months later, a brilliant idea struck me. During my performance, I introduced an illusion involving a small blue box containing a cube with different colored sides: red, white, purple, blue, green, and yellow.

I would ask a spectator to secretly choose a color, place it face up in the box, and replace the cover. Astonishingly, I would reveal the chosen color, reading their mind accurately.

Inspired by this, I contacted the craftsman who made my blue pocket square and inquired if he could create a similar piece that could glow in various colors. After three prototypes, and an investment of $800, my new magical assistant, Henry (Hank for short), was born.

Hank A. Kerchief, wanting into my act, would now accurately glow in the color that the spectator had selected, and soon became one of my signature tricks.

People often inquired about Hank, and magicians even expressed interest in having one themselves. I humorously responded that Hank was an only child, always eliciting a good laugh.

Orson Bean, John and Henry

A New Magical Perspective

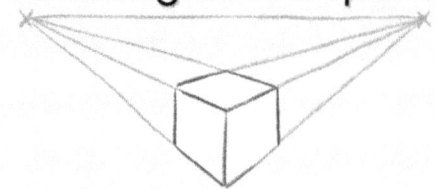

Through these experiences, I realized the power I held in influencing people's perceptions and transforming negatives into positives. Engaging in impromptu magic performances four nights a week, I caught the attention of a fellow magician who offered me a valuable piece of advice after observing my act. He advised me to focus on making the spectator the hero of the illusion. This feedback sparked a realization within me, prompting me to shift my perspective and approach to magic performances.

From that moment onwards, I shifted my magic perspective toward empowering the audience to create magical moments. This approach significantly enhanced audience reactions. By making them the focal point and involving them, I could connect with them on a more engaging level. Showing genuine interest in their individuality made a remarkable impact on my magic performances.

Occasionally, I noticed some audience members getting distracted by my appearance, hindering their enjoyment of the magic. To address this, I conducted an experiment. I began my shows by introducing myself, sharing a personal tidbit. I recounted my experience with a brain tumor in 2002, leading to a change in my facial features due to surgery.

Following this revelation, I paused, observing the audience eagerly awaiting more details. I teased softly, hinting at my newfound ability to influence thoughts. Transitioning into a mentalism act, I showcased a card trick involving a spectator's mind, leaving them astounded by the finale.

This approach initiated a connection with the audience by sharing something personal. It also addressed the unspoken question they likely had in mind. By explaining the reason behind my facial paralysis, and getting that out of the way, I allowed them to fully focus on my magic performance. It was a powerful realization that I could shift the focus of the conversation.

During interactions with guests, especially groups of women, magic would unfold. Sitting at a six foot green felted table, I would draw guests in to witness close-up magic. Initially, women seated beside me appeared reserved due to my facial condition. However, as I performed and shared personal anecdotes, I noticed a shift in their body language. They would relax, uncross their legs and arms, lean forward, smile, and become more engaged as the magic unfolded. Many times, these same women would ask to hug me at the end of my performances.

Having a blast in the Close-up Gallery

Picture courtesy of Taylor Wong - Magic Castle Photographer

This started to build my confidence, that I was worthy of being appreciated and loved, despite my paralyzed face. These women started to feel comfortable and let their guards down, knowing that I would never try to do anything inappropriate. I came to understand how women tend to feel in today's society and are on constant guard against inapropriate advances. Once I made that special bond, they started to share their femininity. It's like I empowered them to be vulnerable again. What a gift. After hundreds of such interactions, I started to heal.

We're all fearful of the unknown. Sometimes our fears stop us in our tracks. Here are some thoughts to help you avoid this trap.

"Your time is limited, so don't waste it living someone else's life. Don't be trapped by dogma - which is living with the results of other people's thinking. Don't let the noise of other's opinions drown out your own inner voice. And most important, have the courage to follow your heart and intuition. They somehow already know what you truly want to become. Everything else is secondary."
- Steve Jobs -

INTERMISSION

Like in all good musicals, the actors and audience need a small break. This is a good time for you to stretch your legs and get something to drink. When you return, you will discover one of those easter eggs I eluded to earlier.

As a magician, I've learned that even simple magic effects can make a profound impression upon the viewer.

Let me teach you a magic trick, which will help you make a lasting first impression when making a new aquaintance.

Imagine handing your business card to a new client and making it float between your fingers. It has been my experience that the recipients tend to keep the card, as they saw it do something magical.

This can also be done with a credit card or rewards card.

If you want to learn the secret to this simple and visual illusion, click the QR code below.

At the end of the video, the intermission bells will ring, signaling the beginning of the next act.

PEARLS OF WISDOM
Developing a Magic Mindset

*" I think anything is possible if you have the mindset
and the will and desire to do it and put the time in."*
- Roger Clemens -

In our everyday lives, we often focus on what's real and practical. But what if we could see the world differently? A "magic mindset" helps us do just that. This way of thinking allows us to see possibilities, be creative, and find joy in the little things. In this section, we'll explore what a magic mindset is, why it's important, and how to develop it in our lives.

What is a Magic Mindset?

A magic mindset is about believing in the wonderful possibilities around us. It means looking at life with a sense of wonder and imagination. Instead of seeing problems as big barriers, we can view them as exciting challenges to overcome. This mindset helps us to:

- Be Creative - When we think magically, we allow ourselves to dream big and come up with new ideas.

- Stay Curious - A magic mindset encourages us to ask questions and explore the world around us.

- Be Strong - Instead of giving up when things are tough, we learn to bounce back and keep going.

- Appreciate Life - We learn to be thankful for even the small, beautiful moments in our day.

- Trust Our Feelings - We listen to our inner voice and follow what feels right for us.

Why is a Magic Mindset Important?

Having a magic mindset can change how we experience life. Here are some benefits:

- Boosts Creativity - Thinking magically helps us come up with new and exciting ideas. This is useful in school, work, and personal projects.

- Makes Problem-Solving Easier - When we face challenges with curiosity, we can find better solutions.

- Improves Relationships - A magic mindset helps us connect with others and build stronger friendships.

- Increases Happiness - By noticing the magic in our lives, we feel more joy and satisfaction.

- Builds Resilience - We learn to keep trying, even when things don't go our way.

How to Develop a Magic Mindset

Here are some simple ways to build a magic mindset:

- Practice Being Present - Take a few moments each day to focus on the present. Breathe deeply and notice what's around you. This helps you see the beauty in everyday life.

- Keep a Journal - Write down your thoughts, dreams, and things you are grateful for. This can help you recognize the magic in your experiences.

- Be Playful - Allow yourself to have fun! Play games, draw, or try new activities. Being playful helps spark your creativity.

- Try New Things - Step outside your comfort zone. Explore new hobbies, meet new people, or visit different places. New experiences can open your mind to new possibilities.

- Create an Inspiring Space - Surround yourself with things that make you feel happy and inspired, like uplifting books, art, or photos.

- Set Daily Intentions - Each morning, think about what you want to achieve and how you want to feel. This can help guide your actions throughout the day.

- Practice Gratitude - Take time to appreciate the good things in your life. Remember to say thank you for the little moments that bring you joy.

———————————————

A magic mindset allows us to see the world in a new light. It helps us be more creative, curious, and resilient. Practicing the steps outlined here, we can learn to find magic in our daily lives.

With a magic mindset, we can turn ordinary moments into extraordinary ones and live a life filled with joy and wonder. So let's start believing in the magic around us!

Deep in thought at The Magic Castle, surrounded by caricatures of master magicians

Picture courtesy of Ryan Palmieri

ACT 13

Learning from a Master

" The beautiful thing about learning is that no one can take it away from you."
- B.B. King -

When I first ventured into the enchanting world of magic as a young boy, my aim was straightforward: to dazzle the audience! Little did I know that incorporating a personal story into my tricks was the real magic ingredient. Fast forward to my debut at The Castle in 2007, where I discovered the formula for awe and wonder. I collected magic tricks like a squirrel hoarding acorns, eagerly awaiting that spark of creativity to ignite.

One day, a classic money trick reminded me of family game nights filled with Monopoly. A lightbulb moment! Why not transform Monopoly money into the real thing? By creating my own Monopoly-sized bills, I intertwined cherished memories of Sunday game sessions with my family into an illusion. Suddenly, my magic transcended mere tricks; it became a nostalgic journey back to the carefree days of childhood.

Blending various tricks has become my hallmark, creating unique performances that captivate and mesmerize audiences.

Monopoly money to real money

Picture courtesy of Taylor Wong - Magic Castle Photographer

Then, I had the opportunity to attend a workshop led by the amazing magician Joshua Jay. We connected like two peas in a pod. I invited Josh to be my VIP guest at my show at The Castle that evening, and it turned out to be a huge success! His reaction? An astounding 24 gasps of awe from the audience in just one show! He was truly impressed by the magical moments I crafted. Thus, a wonderful friendship was formed!

One of his newest magic acts was called "Balance." Picture a water bottle, toothbrush, pencil, deck of cards, and a box of crayons all defying gravity in a stunning spectacle. I was so enchanted by the illusion that I grabbed one as soon as it became available. I added my own twist, incorporating it into my personal story of recovery from brain surgery, which had thrown my sense of balance off-kilter.

My Balance Illusion finale

Picture courtesy of Ryan Palmieri

Fast forward to the following August at the Magic Live convention. While filming my documentary, I gathered the courage to ask Josh if I could present my version of his trick on camera.

Off we went to Vegas, where the convention's producer graciously allowed us to film the interview with Josh after hours. The entire scene unfolded in front of Josh's Vanishing Inc. booth.

Picture of John and Joshua Jay courtesy of Ryan Palmieri

"You know, John, I've seen thousands of different versions of Balance and they are all kind of derivative of my story. This is the best I've ever seen of someone taking it and making it completely their own. So, thanks! It's a special thrill for me to see someone take something I've worked so hard on and plus it, and make it even better!"
- Josh Jay -

Joshua Jay Live at Carnegie Hall - Courtesy of Joshua Jay

Josh has been so supportive of my magic journey. When he announced that he was performing an all new show at Carnegie Hall, I immediately bought a front row center seat and booked my trip to be there to support him.

With Josh at Carnegie Hall

ACT 14

TED Talk and Documentary

"Being Different is Your Superpower."
- John David Kippen -

At this moment, I felt the confidence and drive to share my journey, realizing that magic needed to be an integral part of it. I reached out to my good friend, David Blatter, an incredible magician who has appeared on shows like Fool Us and America's Got Talent. I asked for his assistance in creating a new magic act that would blend with motivational speaking. He emphasized that, if I wanted to be a motivational speaker, I needed credibility, and suggested I consider doing a TEDx talk. I hadn't thought about it, but I was open to the idea.

David kindly submitted two applications on my behalf to events at UCLA and San Diego State University. Both were seeking speakers for ten available slots. Just two weeks later, I received an email from the organizer of the San Diego event requesting more information. After several conversations, they informed me there were three openings left, and they wanted me to fill one of them.

Excited, I shared this wonderful news with my friends on social media. My long-time friend, Ryan Palmieri, called to express his interest in producing a documentary about my story. Flattered, I enthusiastically agreed to produce the film. He also asked if he could film the preparation for the TEDx talk. I contacted the event organizer for permission, and since it would provide them with greater exposure, they happily agreed.

The event was scheduled in three months, and I quickly realized I had yet to prepare a speech. I spent the following weeks crafting my presentation, and I must admit, I needed help.

A friend from The Castle, Michael Varna, who is a professional writer, with experience in crafting TED talks, lent his expertise. After several drafts, I submitted the speech to the event organizer. She responded positively, saying it was fantastic, and couldn't wait to see me on stage.

With Good Friend David Blatter

The arduous memorization phase began. After two months, I had the script memorized and asked the organizer if I could come down to walk the stage. Having performed in front of large audiences before, I understood that familiarity with the space would help me focus more on my delivery. The organizer mentioned that this wasn't necessary, but I replied, "Maybe not for you, but it is for me." We arranged a visit three weeks before the event

David and I drove to San Diego to check out the venue. With my extensive theatrical experience, both on stage and behind the scenes, I requested a meeting with the lighting and sound technicians. As I walked the stage, I shared some preferences for how I wanted to be lit. I could feel the excitement from the organizer and the technicians, realizing that I was contributing to the event's success. The organizer asked if I would be willing to go first, as the other speakers were hesitant. I happily accepted.

Picture of Dennis and Bob Fitch courtesy of Ryan Palmieri

I collaborated with Ryan and David, and we decided to take the train from Van Nuys to San Diego, planning to do some filming the day before the event. My close friends, Dennis and Bob Fitch, offered to come down to support me, while Ryan brought along his friend Ignacio to serve as a second cameraman. Things were finally starting to feel real.

When we arrived at the hotel the night before the event, I asked the front desk if there was a room available for rehearsal, since I was scheduled to give a TEDx talk the next day. The desk staff wasn't sure, as the events manager had left for the weekend. Fortunately, the hotel manager overheard and kindly offered us one of their meeting rooms.

After enjoying dinner together, we began our rehearsal. This was the first time I actually delivered the speech, which included a magic effect in the middle. After a few hours of practice, everything started to click.

Picture of David Blatter and Bob Fitch courtesy of Ryan Palmieri

I am deeply grateful to my friend, Bob Fitch, for his invaluable assistance in preparing for this talk. Bob began his career as an actor on Broadway, starring in the inaugural production of the musical *Annie*. When he wasn't on stage, he was performing magic and has since become one of the world's most renowned magic consultants, collaborating with famous magicians like David Copperfield. I feel incredibly fortunate that Bob agreed to mentor me.

Everything seemed to fall into place. I finally felt confident that I could successfully deliver this presentation. That night, I went to bed feeling both relieved and excited for the adventure awaiting me the next day.

The following morning, I arrived at the venue well ahead of schedule. The lighting crew was busy focusing the lights on the stage. Spotting an opportunity to enhance the event's aesthetic, I placed my bags and coat on a front-row chair and made my way onto the stage. I noticed a technician in a lift, trying to adjust the lights, and I offered my assistance. I anticipated that the event organizer would come over and tell me, "John, we've got this. Just head back to the dressing room and relax until it's time." To my surprise, she didn't.

Helping to focus the Stage Lights at TEDx

Picture courtesy of Ryan Palmieri

It seemed she recognized my lighting expertise could contribute to the event's success, and allowed me to take charge. In my element, having lit countless shows before, we added backlighting, adjusted the front lights, and incorporated some color. Everything started to look impressive. I went backstage to get dressed and unwind, preparing for the event to start. The stage featured a three-foot-tall TEDx prop and a six-foot red carpet circle at its center, flanked by twenty-foot screens on either side. Above the stage, I would be projected so that all 800 attendees could see me and my slides clearly.

Approximately five minutes before the event began, the MC came backstage to meet with me. I realized that if the MC felt enthusiastic about my speech, it would energize the audience as well. Just before he took the stage, I performed a quick magic trick, transforming Monopoly money into real cash. This got him pumped up for my introduction. Taking the stage, I was welcomed by a warm and excited crowd. The house lights were dimmed, so I could only see the first two rows, but I could make out a few familiar faces of friends who had driven down to surprise me. It felt like I was surrounded by friends, and I was at ease on stage; it brought back wonderful memories of performing in high school and college. I was sharing my story with an audience of over 800 people.

Deftly delivering my TED Talk

Picture courtesy of Ryan Palmieri

I was more thrilled than nervous. As the audience began to laugh and respond to my speech, I felt completely at home. Everything was going smoothly, until about three-quarters of the way through my presentation, when the front lights suddenly dimmed. I looked up and exclaimed, "Oh!" Luckily, they returned to full brightness within about five seconds.

I paused, glanced at the audience, raised my hands, and whispered, "Magic." The crowd erupted in laughter and applause. I concluded my speech to a standing ovation, feeling incredibly happy.

As I made my way off the stage toward the dressing room, the organizer apologized for the lighting mishap and said that they would edit that part out of the video for the TEDx website. I replied, "Don't you dare! That was one of my finest moments." She smiled and said, "Alright, we'll keep it in."

As we headed back home, it began to sink in that my exciting journey as a professional speaker had officially begun.

My talk has now transitioned from a TEDx event to a full TED talk, and you can easily find it by searching for my name on the ted.com website. It has already been viewed over a million times and continues to grow.

"The name's Kippen, John Kippen"

Picture courtesy of Ryan Palmieri

Picture courtesy of Ryan Palmieri

John's
Ultimate
Illusion

Act 14 | Scene | 2

After the TED Talk wrapped up, Ryan and I turned our attention to the documentary. My co-stars included my magic mentor, Bob Fitch, my partner in crime, David Blatter, and several of my magic supporters. Additionally, my friend Ron Charmichel, who appears in one of my stories about the healing powers of magic, also made a cameo appearance.

I remember being at Jamie Lee's home, working on her computer, when I shared that my friend Ryan had proposed filming a documentary about my life, particularly focusing on my recovery after brain surgery. An uncomfortable silence followed. I felt hesitant to ask Jamie if she would participate in the film. Although I was fixated on the computer screen, I could still feel her intense gaze. Finally, she broke the silence with, "... and?" I took this as a sign to proceed. Looking her in the eyes, I asked, "Jamie, would you please be in the film?" Her enthusiastic reply was a resounding "F... yes!" Once again, Jamie demonstrated her belief in me. I expressed my gratitude and assured her that I would share the great news with Ryan, and that we would soon reach out with a shooting schedule.

I got into my car and reflected on everything. It was at that moment, I realized the documentary was destined to be something special. The budget had skyrocketed, but I didn't mind; this was an incredible, once-in-a-lifetime opportunity. I understood that the investment would be worthwhile. I immediately called Ryan to share the fantastic news. Now it was time to roll up our sleeves and get to work.

Everything began to come together seamlessly. A client of mine, Scott Webley, owned a set of sound stages in The Valley. I reached out to him and shared the project's details. He kindly offered his facility for filming several scenes.

Being interviewed for the documentary

Picture courtesy of Ryan Palmieri

Additionally, we received permission from the Board of Directors to shoot at The Magic Castle, for which I am eternally grateful.

We also utilized various other locations throughout Los Angeles. However, it was Jamie who truly took the film to the next level. She spoke about me as both a person and an artist, sharing my challenges alongside my achievements, which allowed the audience to connect with me on a more profound level.

Jamie, in the Dai Vernon Corner of The Magic Castle,
filming the documentary

Picture courtesy of Ryan Palmieri

Once filming concluded, I entrusted the editing of the project to my friend and computer client, Rob Lawe, and his team.

Within a month, we had a rough cut ready. Rob did an incredible job condensing countless hours of footage into a concise 15-minute documentary, now titled *"John's Ultimate Illusion."*

I chose to submit the completed film to four film festivals, the most notable being Doc LA. To my astonishment, it won the award for Best Inspirational Documentary of the Year.

When I shared the news of the award with Jamie, she enthusiastically agreed to join me at the ceremony, and even offered to present the award to me. The film festival organizer was thrilled by this arrangement. You can view the award presentation by scanning the code on the following page.

I am deeply thankful to Jamie for her kindness and support; she will forever hold a cherished spot in my heart.

Jamie presenting me an award at DOC LA Film Festival

Picture courtesy of Peter Huh

"Mommy would only come out for someone like John Kippen... I truly believe, John, even though it's an incredibly difficult aspect of your life, it's the greatest opportunity because of what it's given you, which in turn you have given to all of us. Through you, we are all better. I couldn't love you more and I couldn't be prouder of the journey you've taken as an artist through adversity and that you are living your best life now."
- Jamie Lee Curtis -

PEARLS OF WISDOM
Putting Others First

In life, we often focus on our own desires and needs. However, putting others first can sometimes yield the greatest rewards. This involves caring for those around us and making them feel valued, which can significantly enhance their day and foster stronger connections.

Listen to Others

One of the easiest ways to prioritize others is by truly listening to them. When a friend shares their troubles, take the time to engage attentively. Show your concern by nodding and asking questions. This approach makes them feel appreciated and heard. Often, people simply need someone who is willing to listen.

Offer Help When Possible

If you notice someone in distress, extend your help. Whether it's a classmate needing assistance with their homework or a neighbor struggling with heavy bags, small acts of kindness can leave a lasting impact. Supporting others not only aids them but also brings joy to ourselves.

Share Your Belongings

Sharing is another meaningful way to demonstrate care. If you possess something a friend would like to use, such as a book or a toy, don't hesitate to share it. This simple gesture can bring happiness and appreciation to your friend. Furthermore, sharing cultivates a sense of community and connection.

Use Kind Words

The language and tone we choose can significantly influence those around us. Always aim to speak with kindness and uplift your friends. Compliment their achievements or offer comforting words during tough times. A few encouraging words can brighten someone's day and elevate their spirits.

Give Your Time

Time is one of the most precious gifts we can offer. Make an effort to spend time with friends and family, especially when they need your support. Whether it's enjoying games, taking a stroll, or simply being together, your presence can have a significant impact. Remember, it's not about the quantity of time, but the quality of those moments.

Understand Their Feelings

Try to empathize by putting yourself in someone else's position. If your friend is feeling down, consider how they might be experiencing their emotions. Show empathy by saying something like, "I'm sorry you're facing this." Recognizing and validating their feelings can provide them with support.

Celebrate Their Successes

When someone you know achieves something significant, take the time to celebrate their success alongside them! Whether it's a good grade, a job promotion, or any other achievement, express your joy for them. This demonstrates that you value their happiness and take pride in their work.

Putting others first doesn't mean neglecting your own needs; rather, it's about achieving balance. By caring for others, we foster a world filled with kindness and support. Keep in mind that the more we prioritize others, the more joy and love we cultivate in our own lives and those around us.

ACT 15

Going the Extra Mile

" There are no traffic jams along the extra mile."
- Zig Ziglar -

One of my favorite themes in magic is when a freely chosen card vanishes then reappears in an impossible location. The question is, how far is the magician willing to go in order to achieve a mindblowing magical mystery?

As part of my standard set, I ask a spectator to select a card and sign it. This card later appears in a sealed envelope, inside a zippered compartment of my wallet.

One time, I entertained a delightful group of ladies at The Magic Castle, where they showed great enthusiasm. After my performance, they revealed themselves as medical students from UCLA. During a relaxed chat at the bar, they curiously asked about my face, to which I calmly shared my experience with a brain tumor and recovery.

Having a medical background, this sparked their interest. Of course, I didn't mind the attention from such a pleasant group of women. Time passed quickly as we engaged in lengthy conversations. Eventually, a Castle manager interrupted us, signaling the club's closing time at 1:00 am.

As we bid farewell, I secretly overheard them planning a stop at In-N-Out Burger on Sunset Blvd on their way home. This sparked a daring idea in me. Earlier in the evening, during my performance, Courtney had chosen and signed the 8 of Hearts for my Card to Wallet Routine.

I retrieved the signed card. In a spur of the moment decision, I grabbed the card and headed out the back exit, waiting patiently in my car.

Courtney and her friends prior to leaving the Castle

A few minutes later, the group exited the Castle and got in their car. As they headed down the driveway, I slowly followed. Fortunately, it was dark outside so they didn't notice me.

Sure enough, they headed for the In-N-Out Burger on Sunset and got in the drive thru. I was right behind them. As I approached the window to order, I handed the nice lady a ten dollar bill for her trouble and asked if she would run up to the pickup window and place Courtney's Eight of Hearts in the In-N-Out bag that the girls were about to receive.

I went home that night quite content, smiling to myself, just imagining the stunned reactions when they discovered Courtney's card in their bag of burgers!

Sure enough, the next day, a post appeared on my Facebook page, from Courtney: "WTF John!?! How did you get the my card in the bag?"

Along with her FB post, Courtney even sent me a photo as proof, exclaiming, "NFW...How on earth is this possible?"

And perhaps more amazing is that the story doesn't end there...

Six months later, a friend and I were enjoying lunch at a local sushi bar when I noticed a gentleman at the table next to us staring at me, as if he recognized me. Given my facial paralysis, I had grown accustomed to people looking at me, so I brushed it off. A few moments later, he leaned in and said, "Excuse me, this might sound a bit strange, but... are you the In and Out magician?"

I was taken aback! It turned out he had heard the story from one of Courtney's friends. With our tables being so close, he couldn't help but overhear our conversation about magic. Coupled with my facial paralysis, he made the connection that I was the magician, and he was right!

I often ponder how many hundreds of people might have heard that story through word of mouth and imagined what it would be like to find their own signed card nestled in a bag of burgers and fries.

I have learned that going the extra mile to create an unforgetable illusion can make all the difference in creating a once-in-a-lifetime experience.

Magic has the power to do more than just entertain; it can educate, inspire, motivate, and sometimes even heal.

I discovered the ability of magic to help me overcome challenges. Interacting with a group at The Magic Castle a few years ago made me realize that magic has the potential to inspire others to progress in their own lives.

The next few stories demonstrate how performing magic, coupled with my story of my triumph over adversity, gave spectators some insights into how they could deal with serious medical issues, themselves.

During a visit to The Magic Castle, a gentleman named Joe Mansolino recognized me from a previous performance and expressed his group's appreciation for my Close-up Gallery act. Although I wasn't scheduled to perform in the gallery that week, I offered to share some magic with his friends.

One of my preferred spots at The Castle is the Jack Oakie Gallery, also recognized as the classroom. This intimate space is perfect for engaging with a small to medium-sized audience, featuring cozy chairs that could be arranged near the performance table. The lighting is adjustable and provides a pleasant ambiance.

A noteworthy aspect of this space was its privacy, as it was tucked in a quiet hallway off the inner circle. Performances in this area typically began between 7 and 8 pm, creating a serene setting that allowed me to present my magic tricks, and share inspiring anecdotes, without disruptions from loud noises or large crowds.

Ron & Sherri Carmichael, Krystle & Joe Mansolino

While on our way to the Oakie Gallery for my show, Joe confided in me that his friend Ron Carmichael, who was visiting the Castle for the first time that evening, had received news from his doctor that his cancer had recurred for the third time. Ron's initial diagnosis was in 2010, and this was his third battle with the disease.

Joe mentioned that convincing Ron to join them that night was a struggle, as Ron just wanted to stay home and rest. Eventually, Ron agreed to come along and, during the drive to the Castle, expressed that he was overwhelmed by the idea of fighting cancer again and had chosen not to pursue further treatments.

Having been diagnosed with blood cancer, Ron's doctors had outlined a demanding treatment plan involving multiple rounds of chemotherapy. Even though I had just met Ron that evening, his demeanor indicated that he was feeling low and would have preferred to be at home with his wife and friends.

Upon learning about Ron's situation, my goal was to ensure that the group enjoyed themselves and could focus on something magical and engaging. Little did I know what was about to unfold.

During my 45-minute show, I shared my own post-surgery challenges and how magic performances served as my therapy. The shared experience of facing health obstacles created a connection between Ron and I. I hoped that witnessing my performance would offer Ron a new perspective on his challenges. I tailored most of the acts toward Ron to allow him to participate firsthand.

After the show ended, they kindly invited me to join them for dinner and I ended up spending the rest of the evening with my newfound friends. I talked about my journey and how performing had helped me answer the common question: "Why is my face paralyzed?" I explained that audiences had accepted the answer, allowing me to focus on my magic and stories without any distractions.

During dinner, I sat next to Ron on my right side to ensure he spoke into my good ear. My aim for the evening was to engage Ron and take his mind off his diagnosis. I inquired about his life, and he shared that he grew up in Culver City, CA, where he had lived his entire life. He mentioned meeting his friend Joe in grade school in the early 1970s, and they had been best friends since then. In October 2013, Ron married his wife, Sherri, despite battling two forms of cancer. It was evident how much he loved her and their special bond. Ron then asked about my story.

I shared about my life-threatening brain tumor in June 2002 and how the successful surgery left its mark.

After my face was paralyzed, I secluded myself from life for nearly 12 years. However, I discovered that performing magic not only helped me overcome isolation but also brought joy to others, providing a brief distraction from their worries.

During a conversation with Ron, I mentioned my application for a TEDx talk at SDSU. I expressed my hope to be selected as one of the few speakers to share my message, "Being Different is Your Superpower." Our discussion led to an enduring friendship.

The following day, Joe unexpectedly informed me that Ron, on the way home to Culver City, had decided to fight his illness. He requested Sherri to arrange his treatments.

Months later, I received two significant calls in quick succession. The first was from the SDSU Tedx organizer, notifying me of my selection as one of the five speakers for their event. The second call was from Ron, sharing the news of his remission after a short period of treatment.

I often recount the inspiring story of Ron Carmichael, and included it in my TEDx talk. As I revealed his cancer-free status to over 800 attendees, they erupted in applause. I also invited Ron to be part of my documentary film, "*John's Ultimate Illusion*," to which he enthusiastically agreed.

With good friend Ron Carmichael

Making the
Decision to No Longer Hide

You never know when unexpected events will come your way and bring everything to a halt.

Unbeknownst to me at the time, sharing my journey began to empower and inspire audiences. In this piece, I recount a special encounter with a woman named Daryn.

On a bustling Saturday evening, I sat at the Castle's Palace Bar, observing the crowd. Always on the lookout for groups interested in close-up magic. My attention was drawn to a woman approaching the staircase to the Inner Circle. Clad in black, with baggy clothes and a hat reminiscent of the Wicked Witch from "The Wizard of Oz," she seemed lost in thought as she walked down the hallway.

As I greeted her, with, "Hi, how are you?," she paused, giving me a surprised look that seemed to convey, "Please, just let me be." She then proceeded toward the staircase. Without hesitation, I followed her downstairs and caught up with the rest of her group.

My sole purpose at the Castle was to entertain. Spotting what seemed to be the leader among the small group of 5 or 6 guests, I inquired if they were enjoying themselves. The leader acknowledged the Castle's charm but seemed unsure of what to do next.

Upon learning they hadn't witnessed any captivating close-up magic that evening, I suggested we move to one of the impromptu performance tables. As we settled in, I requested the woman in black to sit to my right, while the rest of the group took the remaining chairs.

Introducing myself, I learned that the lady beside me was Daryn. From our earlier interaction, it was evident that she wasn't having the best time. My goal for that performance was simple - to make Daryn smile, nothing more.

To achieve this, I placed her at the center of attention. Each magic trick I performed revolved around Daryn, making her the star of the show. Within minutes, I observed a change in her demeanor. Gradually, a smile began to grace her face.

She removed her peculiar hat and made eye contact with me, perhaps signaling the worries she carried that evening were dissipating as she relished the attention and moments of wonder. My intention was beginning to take shape.

Upon wrapping up my 30-minute presentation, it was evident all of them were thoroughly enjoying themselves. Unlike most audiences who would typically applaud, express gratitude, and move on, this group remained seated, eager for more.

I proceeded to recount how magic had been a lifeline for me, helping me embrace my facial paralysis. Not only did I come to terms with it, but I also learned to even celebrate it. I vividly described the pivotal moment when I stopped shying away from life by avoiding mirrors and dodging photographs.

Rarely do we recall the precise moment of our epiphany, the instant when we realize unfounded fears were hindering us from pursuing our aspirations.

Upon sharing my story, Daryn stood up and gestured for me to do the same. She then embraced me tightly, a hug that left a lasting impression, akin to reuniting with a long-lost sibling. This unexpected gesture took me by surprise. Despite having just met her, she held on to me as if her life depended on it. Naturally, I reciprocated with an equally heartfelt hug. In that moment, we shared a connection that was yet to unfold.

After what felt like minutes but was probably only 30 seconds, she stepped back, tears welling in her eyes, and said, "John, I need to tell you something."

"Four years ago, I underwent a double mastectomy due to the BRCA1 gene. Following my mother, aunt, and sister, I was the last in my family to face this surgery." She explained how engrossed she was in my performance and how much she enjoyed the magic in the moment.

It wasn't until I shared my journey of overcoming the fear of public exposure and embracing my true self that she realized we shared similar paths.

With all of us as witnesses, she made a promise to herself to stop hiding. Overwhelmed, I sank back into my chair. She excused herself to compose herself in the restroom.

One of her college friends, who had supported Daryn since her surgery four years ago, witnessed this transformative moment. In just 30 minutes, I accomplished what Daryn and her friends had been attempting for the past four years.

When I initially offered to perform for Daryn and her friends, my only goal was to entertain them and bring a smile to Daryn's face. It wasn't long before I realized the transformative impact of magic when coupled with a genuine story of overcoming challenges.

Ladies and gentlemen, we all possess the extraordinary ability to alter someone's view of their life's purpose by sharing our passions openly and wholeheartedly.

"Face your deficiencies and acknowledge them; but do not let them master you. Let them teach you patience, sweetness and insight."
- Helen Keller -

Performing for a Vegas Headliner

It was just another Monday night at The Castle. I sat calmly at the Palace performance table as the last main stage show concluded.

A couple took a seat at my table. The gentleman seemed oddly familiar, but I couldn't quite place him. To close the show, I presented my signature signed card to wallet routine.

His companion, Robyn, picked and signed the two of hearts, which, later ended up sealed in an envelope in my wallet. When the performance wrapped up, the gentleman introduced himself as Paul Zerdin.

Paul had won *America's Got Talent* in 2015 with his ventriloquist act. He and his fiancée, Robyn Mellor, were at the Castle that evening to support a friend performing in the Palace Show.

Since it was late and most guests had already departed, we lingered at the table, chatting. I had often been curious about what it was like to audition and perform on AGT. Paul shared his experiences from competing on *America's Got Talent* and later performing on the main stage at the Planet Hollywood Hotel in Las Vegas.

We spoke for about an hour before they mentioned they needed to leave for a rehearsal at noon the following day. Their plan was to head back to their hotel for a quick nap before packing and taking the short flight to Las Vegas.

After walking them downstairs and bidding farewell, I got into my car and drove home.

On the way, a wild idea struck me: what if, when Robyn arrived at her dressing room for the noon rehearsal, she discovered her signed two of hearts taped to the mirror? Could this be my ultimate card to impossible location illusion?

My mind began to race. After getting home around 1:30 a.m., I started digging into information about Paul. I discovered that he was represented by an agent at the Creative Artists Agency in New York. I sent an email to his agent outlining my idea and then went to bed, hoping to wake up to a response with suggestions on how to bring this illusion to life.

Picture Licensed through Alamy.com

However, when I checked my email at 7 a.m., I found no reply from his agent. Undeterred, I turned to Google and learned that Harrah's Entertainment also managed the entertainment for Planet Hollywood.

I called the Harrah's hotel and requested to speak with their entertainment director. After a few rings, a man picked up who was responsible for entertainment at Planet Hollywood. With confidence, I shared my bold idea with him. He expressed enthusiasm but mentioned that he couldn't assist directly. He explained that the Paul Zerdin show had its own production team, and he was not involved with them.

Nonetheless, he kindly provided me with the name of the show's director and the phone number of his assistant, suggesting she might be able to help. I thanked him and reached out to the assistant.

When she answered, she sounded quite puzzled. I suspect she was a younger, less experienced team member who did not fully grasp the significance of the trick I was proposing. She took my contact information and promised to relay my message to the show's director.

I ended the call feeling disheartened and on the verge of giving up. My ideas had run dry, and time was slipping away. If they didn't find the card before the rehearsal, the illusion wouldn't have the desired impact. I didn't want Robyn to discover the card after 24-48 hours, as she might assume I sent it via FedEx, which wouldn't feel very magical.

Thirty minutes later, my phone rang—it was the director himself. We chatted briefly, and he expressed his enthusiasm for my idea. He mentioned that if I could get the card to the Planet Hollywood box office, a crew member would retrieve it, place it on the mirror, and send me a photo. I thanked him and hung up, feeling hopeful as he wished me good luck.

Suddenly, the illusion seemed possible again. I glanced at my watch: it was 10 AM, and the rehearsal was set to start in two hours. Time was of the essence. Without hesitation, I jumped into my car, card in hand, and drove to the nearest airport. It was a 20-minute journey to the cargo section at Bob Hope Burbank Airport, where I could send a package on a flight.

However, as I parked and stepped out of the car, I realized I had forgotten my wallet at home in my rush. I only had a photo of my ID on my phone and around $30 in my center console. At this point, my only option was to engage the airport employee in the success of my cunning plan.

I had nothing to lose but everything to gain!

I entered the building and walked up to a counter that resembled my local bank, complete with a wall of bulletproof glass and a small slot. Behind the glass stood an employee who appeared quite uninterested. Beyond him were a set of swinging doors leading out to the tarmac. Burbank is a commuter airport where passengers step onto the tarmac and ascend a staircase that rolls away once the plane is ready for takeoff. I approached the window and inquired about the gentleman's name.

Picture of Paul Zerdin and Robyn Mellor Licensed through Alamy.com

He introduced himself as James. I realized that for my plan to succeed, I needed to engage James in the success of this ruse. I asked him to envision Robyn's reaction when she found her card, which she had signed just a few hours earlier, taped to the makeup mirror in her dressing room.

This was post 9/11, so bringing anything onto a plane likely required several forms of ID and a substantial fee. All I had was a picture of my driver's license on my phone and about $30. To prove to James that I was indeed a magician, I performed one of my favorite card tricks, which I always carried with me. His facial expression was one of awe and wonder as the effect concluded.

I asked James if there was any way he could help get Robyn's signed card to Vegas. I told him, the success of the trick was now in his hands and his hands only. He looked around and made sure we were the only two people in the room. After a few seconds, he whispered, "Ok, give me the signed two of hearts."

He quickly took the card and sealed it in an envelope, wrote a short note on the back, and told me to wait right there. I watched in amazement as he turned and went out the swinging doors onto the tarmac and climbed the stairs to a Southwest Airlines jet bound for Vegas. He handed the envelope to a flight attendant and returned to the counter as she read the note. I thanked him and said I would mention him by name every time I told this story.

I returned to my car and discovered a courier service in Vegas that would, for $50, pick up the card from the airport and rush it to the box office at Planet Hollywood. About 75 minutes later, I received the following picture. It was just before noon, and the card arrived with just 10 minutes to spare.

"I saw it in the mirror and couldn't believe how it made it from LA to Vegas... It was incredible...
I was completely blown away!"
– Robyn Mellor

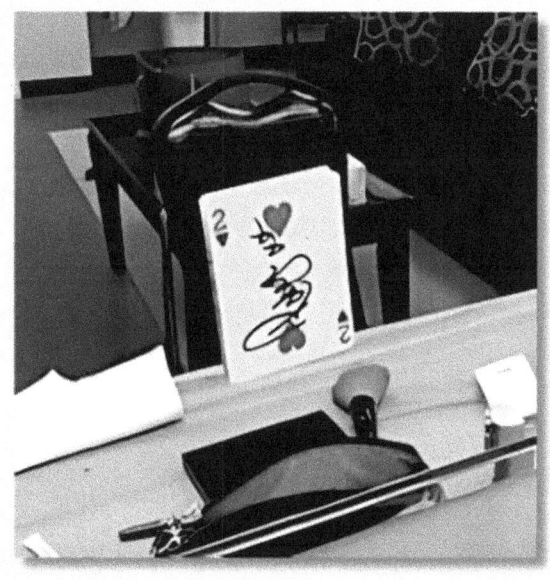

The next day, I received an email from Paul expressing his gratitude and amazement, along with an invitation to meet up the next time they were in Los Angeles.

A couple years later, while I was filming my documentary, both Paul and Robyn eagerly agreed to a Zoom interview. As they recounted their reactions, it was clear that the experience left a lasting impression. Unfortunately, the interview didn't make it into the film, but the story continues.

"I was like, Oh My God! It was something entirely different... We've seen all the magic shows in Vegas, including Copperfield many times, and this is the trick that stands out—it's the only one she talks about!" - Paul Zerdin

What I have learned is when you dare to dream big, the seemingly impossible can become possible. Don't hesitate to take risks; the lessons you gain will be invaluable in the future. You might be surprised at how a complete stranger can become invested in the success of your dreams if you simply share them with the universe.

PEARLS OF WISDOM
The Magic of Risk-Taking

Every day, we face choices. Some decisions are straightforward, such as what to have for breakfast, while others can be more challenging, like trying something completely new. Let's focus on the concept of risk-taking and its significance.

What is Risk-Taking?

Risk-taking involves engaging in actions that may carry the possibility of failure or danger. It can range from something as simple as speaking in front of an audience to something as significant as relocating to a new city. By taking risks, we venture beyond our comfort zones. While this can be intimidating, it often leads to incredible experiences.

Why Take Risks?

Growth: Taking risks allows us to learn more about ourselves. For instance, trying out a new sport might reveal hidden talents, fostering personal growth and boosting self-confidence.

Opportunity: Sometimes, embracing risk can open doors to exciting opportunities. By reaching out to someone for friendship, you may find a lifelong companion. Similarly, applying for a job that seems out of reach could lead to a successful hire!

Overcoming Fear: Taking small risks can help us confront our fears. For example, if heights make you anxious, embarking on a gentle uphill hike can gradually build your courage. Each risk taken strengthens your resilience.

How to Take Risks Safely

Engaging in risk-taking doesn't equate to recklessness. Here are some strategies for taking risks in a safe manner:

Consider Your Options - Before diving into something new, take a moment to contemplate the potential outcomes. What could go right? What might go wrong? This reflection will help you prepare for any outcome.

Take Baby Steps - You don't need to make significant leaps immediately. Begin with small actions. For instance, if you're looking to travel, start with a day trip before planning an entire week away.

Learn From Failures - Not every risk will lead to success. If things don't unfold as expected, don't lose heart. Analyze what occurred and gain insights from it. This is how we evolve.

Let's explore a few individuals who embraced risks:

Thomas Edison - He encountered numerous failures before successfully inventing the light bulb. Each setback imparted valuable lessons, and he persisted without giving up.

Steve Jobs - The co-founder of Apple made daring decisions in product development and marketing, betting on unconventional ideas, changing the face of technology.

Nelson Mandela - Took great risks in the fight against Apartheid in South Africa, enduring many years of imprisonment for his beliefs; ultimately becoming president.

Risk-taking is a vital aspect of life. Although it can be daunting, the potential rewards often surpass the fears involved. By embracing risks, we can learn, grow, and uncover new possibilities. So, the next time you encounter a decision, consider the risks you might take; it could lead to an extraordinary adventure!

ACT 16

Performing for One of My Idols

"Only those who will risk going too far can possibly find out how far one can go."
- T.S. Eliot -

Living and working professionally in LA has given me the chance to perform for numerous celebrities, but one experience was unlike any other. Following my previous Pearls of Wisdom, I decided to throw caution to the wind and take one of the biggest risks of my magic career.

When Alex Trebek revealed his battle with pancreatic cancer, I felt compelled to see if I could bring him some joy through my performance. I had never tried to locate a celebrity for a show before (or anyone else, for that matter!).

Eventually, I managed to contact his daughter, Nicky, and shared my personal story about how magic had transformed my life. My mission had become to spread joy and laughter to those facing medical challenges.

I invited her to bring her father and close family to the Magic Castle as my special guests. While she expressed her gratitude, she politely declined, explaining that Alex was a very private individual who wouldn't feel comfortable around so many strangers at that stage of his life. I understood her concerns and offered to bring the magic to him instead.

She thanked me and mentioned that she would discuss it with Jean, Alex's wife. About two hours later, Nicky called back with exciting news: they were planning a surprise 75th birthday party for Alex in a month and asked if I would perform then. I graciously accepted the invitation.

The next hurdle was significant: I had under a month to create a custom Jeopardy-themed show. Inspired, I crafted a set of props resembling the iconic blue screens with white lettering that I had seen countless times while watching Jeopardy.

Picture Licensed through Alamy.com

I called Nicky and expressed my desire to film a prediction video on the *Jeopardy* set at Sony Studios—a *Confabulation*, of sorts, for those magicians reading this—where I would predict the choices made by party guests. I proposed that I would bring a projector to showcase the video as a grand finale for my performance.

Though Nicky was a bit confused, she agreed to check with the show's executive producer, who happened to be Alex's best friend. He called me to ask a few more questions, and I did my best to provide answers without revealing any secrets. He mentioned he would attend the party and was eager to see the finale.

I managed to persuade my friends, who were directing and filming my documentary, to meet at Sony Studios later that week. The show was on hiatus, so we filmed in the backstage audition area. Fortunately, this set was an exact replica of the contestant podiums. We were given just an hour to set up lights and film, and we completed everything right on time.

I edited the prediction to include an introduction by Johnny Gilbert, complete with the opening graphics and video, typical of a *Jeopardy* episode. Fortunately, I found a recording of Alex speaking with a contestant named John, which added to the authenticity.

I arrived to the party early to set up the projector and close-up table. The show commenced after dinner, just before dessert. I asked Alex to sit at the table and assist me. When the guests started cheering and chanting his name, he agreed to join me at my side. Alex mentioned that he loved close-up magic, so he would be closely observing every move, eager to catch me in action. I embraced the challenge, and we quickly built a friendly rapport.

During the live show, I asked Alex to select a random playing card and discreetly place it in his shirt pocket without revealing it to anyone. Next, I asked him to choose a random guest at the party; he picked his daughter, Emily, to answer one of 50 randomly selected questions.

FINAL PREDICTION

The question she chose was, "Who was your first crush?" To create the Jeopardy effect, I then asked five random guests to choose single-digit numbers that would represent the wager for the Final Jeopardy segment.

Please note that these decisions were made long after I filmed the video on set.

My performance included my signature card to wallet routine. Alex even jokingly threatened to "kick my butt" if the card turned out to be Nicky's signed eight of hearts.

Picture with Alex and Nicky Trebek courtesy of Ryan Palmieri

BIRTHDAY CARD EFFECT

I had recently seen my friend Paul Green perform a Jeopardy-themed act at the Close-up Gallery in the Magic Castle. After the show, I reached out to him for permission to create my own variation of his effect, to which Paul graciously agreed.

After the show, I received a heartfelt standing ovation and felt elated, knowing that the video reveal was yet to come. Once the applause settled, I channeled my inner Steve Jobs and said, "Oh Alex. There's one more thing..." I then dimmed the lights and started the projector.

ALEX TREBEK SHOW

The audience watched in amazement as they saw me on the Jeopardy set predicting that Alex would select his daughter Emily to answer a randomly chosen question about her first crush, to which she replied, "Alex Baez." I then revealed that my Final Jeopardy wager exactly matched the numbers chosen by five random guests at the party

As a final touch, I asked Alex to unveil the playing card he had placed in his pocket at the beginning of the show. He casually pulled out the jack of diamonds, only to be astonished to see that I was also holding the jack of diamonds in the video!

Picture courtesy of Ryan Palmieri

Approximately 20 minutes after I finished packing up my props, something incredible took place. Alex approached me and expressed a desire to chat. We moved into a side room where we sat together, and I had the chance to share my story about how magic had transformed my life.

I was deeply moved by his bravery in openly declaring he was battling the toughest fight of his life, and seeking the thoughts and prayers of his fans. This inspired me to create a new show and perform it for him. We shared a heartfelt embrace, and he told me it was one of the most meaningful gifts he had ever received.

Mission accomplished!

Picture courtesy of Alex Trebek

Making this seemingly impossible show a reality was a collaborative effort and one of the most gratifying projects of my career.

Creating the show took an entire month, along with a significant investment of time and resources. I practiced right up until the night before the event.

———————————•❖— ❖•———————————

"I've always been captivated by close-up magic. For my birthday last year, my family hired John Kippen to entertain us. He is truly one of the finest close-up magicians I've ever encountered!" - Alex Trebek

Special thanks to Nicky and Jean Trebek, Ryan Palmieri, Libby Ward, and Rene Nijman, whose assistance helped make the evening an overwhelming success!

ACT 17

Saying Goodbye

" If there ever comes a day when we can't be together, keep me in your heart. I'll stay there forever."
- Winnie the Pooh -

I had a truly wonderful relationship with both of my parents. Growing up, they wholeheartedly supported every activity and dream I had. While many of my classmates experienced their parents' divorce, I felt unique and special knowing that after 40 years, my parents remained happily married and loved me deeply.

Of course, like any couple, they had their occasional disagreements. My mom had a short temper, but my dad adored her so much that he would always let her have the last word. They were both attorneys; my mom was among the first female public defenders in Los Angeles, while my dad ran a private law practice. I learned a great deal from observing their relationship. The secret to their long lasting relationship was that my dad let my mom wear the pants in the family.

A great example of this dynamic was their weekend football ritual. They loved watching games together and would place a friendly $20 wager on each game. I often heard my mom say to my dad, "Okay, Harold, I'm taking Dallas." It was clear from my dad's expression that he wanted Dallas too. I would watch him pause, take a deep breath, and then say, "Okay, Fran, how many points do I get?" He cared for my mom so much that he always gave her what she wanted, except when it came to the University of Michigan. As my dad's alma mater, that was a sacred choice my mom never dared to challenge.

They both earned good salaries, allowing them to send me to an expensive private school, ensuring we never wanted for anything. Even after losing our home to a landslide, they managed their finances well. I remember a conversation where my parents told me, "John, we invested a lot in your education; consider that your inheritance." They planned to travel the world, spending their money on experiences rather than material possessions. Each year, they enjoyed a month-long trip to Europe. My mom would return with handmade dolls called Santons and a collection of decorative plates.

I vividly recall our weekly phone calls while they were abroad, especially the story of how my dad accidentally ruined another rental car by using the wrong fuel. They documented their adventures with cameras, capturing thousands of memories. My mom was an early adopter of technology, maintaining a detailed diary on her laptop of everything they did, every restaurant they visited, and all the sights they saw.

I fondly recall the days when my dad would come home after having his film developed, bringing with him nearly 1,000 4 x 6 photos. My mom would meticulously add each picture to Pioneer photo albums, one by one. This was a cherished hobby for her, and she relished every moment. To make it easier for me, she would even create a condensed version of the photos, allowing me to enjoy highlights from their trips without sifting through all those images. I still have those albums and occasionally leaf through them, reminiscing about the wonderful times my parents shared.

Around the year 2000, we began to notice the early signs of my dad's dementia. It started with small forgetful moments and misnaming individuals. I took him to a neurologist, and after several scans and tests, we learned he had frontal temporal dementia. This prompted me to research how to support a loved one facing such a difficult illness.

As time went on, I realized that my parents were falling into debt, spending twice as much as they were earning. I assisted them in assessing their financial situation, which ultimately led to the difficult decision to sell their home and file for bankruptcy. Fortunately, my mom had a pension that allowed them to maintain a comfortable lifestyle.

Our last family vacation on the high seas.

The moment I understood the severity of my dad's dementia was during a bankruptcy court hearing when he mistakenly referred to me as Norman instead of John. Norman was his older brother who had passed away a few years prior. My dad's mental decline progressed, and he began exhibiting inappropriate behavior. My mom, who had a quick temper, struggled to accept his condition. I learned to engage with him in his reality rather than trying to pull him into mine, which seemed to ease his anxiety. Sadly, my mom was unable to adopt this approach. She was losing her partner of over 50 years, her true love, and no matter how hard she tried, she found it difficult to come to terms with his new normal.

I had moved my parents into a rental house on my street. My dad enjoyed taking daily walks, exploring the neighborhood, stopping by the local coffee shop, and visiting Smart & Final. He would stroll down the fruit aisle, casually popping grapes into his mouth, and the store employees didn't mind. One day, however, my dad didn't return from his walk. I received a frantic call from my mom, which prompted me to drop everything, hop in my car, and search the neighborhood for him. He was nowhere to be found.

We called the police, and they arrived within half an hour with six squad cars and a helicopter to assist in the search. I rushed home to print flyers with his picture to distribute throughout the area in hopes of finding someone who had seen him. About an hour later, a car pulled up in front of my parents' home, my dad stepped out and the vehicle began to drive away. One of the officers stopped the car and questioned the driver. The kind gentleman explained that he had found my dad in his store, looking disoriented and dehydrated. He had checked my dad's wallet, found his address, and brought him home.

My dad had somehow walked ten miles away, far beyond the area the police were searching. From that point on, we had to install a deadbolt on the front door to prevent him from going out alone, which escalated his dementia. I recall a time when my mom called, saying my dad was in a panic, repeatedly saying, "I've gotta go. I've gotta go." I rushed over to help calm him down, but he had lost the ability to communicate even the simplest ideas, speaking in sentences that felt like a foreign language, which I affectionately dubbed "Kippenese." I managed to get my dad into my car, and we drove slowly to familiar places he frequented. As we turned left, he pointed to a little shopping center, and I pulled in. He couldn't wait to get out of the car and headed straight toward the cleaners.

As an attorney, my dad's wardrobe required dry cleaning, and he had three pairs of pants ready at the cleaners. He walked in, paid with a $20 bill, and returned to the car, regaining his calm demeanor. This inspired me to create a solution. I grabbed my camera and took pictures of everything familiar to him: his glasses, his pen, his pants, and the places he frequented, like the coffee shop, Smart & Final, and the shoe store. I compiled these images into a scrapbook. Whenever he became agitated, he could open it and browse through until he found something recognizable. This helped him to be able to stay with my mom for another year or two. Eventually, we had to place my dad in a facility for people with dementia. Sadly, this also marked the beginning of my mom's decline.

Mom growing frustrated with Dad's Dementia

My mom had always struggled with an eating disorder, and preparing food for my dad provided her with some nutrition. Once he moved out, she essentially stopped eating and became very frail. This deterioration affected her balance, leading to frequent trips and falls. Her bones, weakened by malnutrition, broke easily. It wasn't just her physical health that was failing; her spirit was breaking too.

I often took my mom out for dinner. On one occasion, she shared a story with me that rocked my world. She confided, that in college, she had been a victim of a date rape. She went on to say she never shared that with anyone including her mom, best friend or even my dad. This revelation helped me understand why she was such a private person.

One of the most frightening moments in my life was when I visited my mom after she had broken her elbow. We had rented a hospital bed for her and put it in the living room. During our conversation, she unexpectedly asked, "John, why did you move the kitchen last night?" I was taken aback and replied, "What do you mean?" She explained that when she went to bed, the kitchen was on the left, but now it was on the right. I couldn't believe my ears. I responded, "Mom, are you telling me that while you were sleeping, I organized a team of workers to quietly dismantle the kitchen and relocate it?"

My mom responded, "I don't know how you did it. You're the magician in the family! But why did you do it?"

I helped her into the car and drove to the hospital, unable to bear the thought of her developing dementia and facing the reality of having two parents losing their grasp on sanity. The ER doctors conducted numerous blood tests, and I waited anxiously for the results. When the doctor informed me that my mom's sodium levels were critically low, I felt a wave of relief wash over me. They planned to administer IV fluids gradually to help restore her sodium levels, which were causing her strange behavior.

My mom was convinced she was in the basement of a restaurant, and no matter what I said, I couldn't convince her she was in the hospital. I asked the doctors if she would be admitted overnight, and they confirmed she would, but they were waiting for a room to become available.

I hugged and kissed my mom, reassuring her that I'd see her the next day. The nurses told me that she would be safe, but I couldn't shake the fear of losing my mom to the same illness that had devastated my dad's mind. I returned home, had a beer, and cried myself to sleep.

The following morning, I called my mom's private room, and she picked up the phone. The first thing I asked was, "Mom, how are you feeling?" She replied, "OK." I then inquired, "Where are you?" She responded, "What do you mean? Where am I?" I insisted, "I'm asking you a serious question. Where are you?" She finally said, "I'm in the frikkin' hospital; where do you think I am?" It was at that moment I realized my mom had returned to her normal self. I brought her home, but she was unable to get out of bed and could no longer walk. Concerned, I took her back to the hospital, where they readmitted her.

In just a few days, the doctors could no longer detect a pulse. She continued to breathe, but her body began to stiffen. I realized she was nearing the end. I reached out to Romy, a close college friend, who came to the hospital and stayed with me until my mom passed away.

The following day, I went to see my dad. Although I'm uncertain if he fully grasped my words, he could tell I was deeply distressed. He wrapped his arm around me and offered comfort.

When I shared the news of my mom's passing, my dad and I could only communicate through hand squeezes. As I held his hand, I would squeeze twice, and he would respond with two squeezes and a giggle.

Sharing the news of mom's passing with Dad.

I then squeezed three times and stopped, and he would mimic me, laughing. I could sense that my dad was still in there somewhere. A month later, I received a call from the owner of my dad's board and care facility, informing me that they had rushed him to the hospital overnight due to breathing difficulties. As I hurried to the hospital, I found him in the ICU on a ventilator. Although my dad had a do-not-resuscitate order, the board and care facility failed to inform the hospital.

I spoke with the hospitalist, who had little optimism regarding my dad's chances of recovery. This was New Year's Eve, and we decided to wait until morning to see if he showed any signs of improvement.

The next day, I received a call from the doctor, who shared they had successfully removed him from the ventilator and placed him on an oxygen mask. During halftime of the Rose Bowl game, I went to visit my dad. The nurse informed me that, while his breathing was slow, it was steady.

I wrapped my arms around him and sat on the edge of his bed, expressing my love. As I left the hospital, I turned on the TV so that my dad could watch the game. The nurse looked at me, puzzled, and remarked, "You know your dad is unconscious." I replied that my dad was a huge football fan and had never missed a Rose Bowl game, insisting that he would be watching the second half.

The nurse shrugged and smiled, likely accustomed to stranger requests. The teams playing were Georgia and Oklahoma, and it was a thrilling game that ended after two overtime periods, with Georgia winning by a touchdown. Just two minutes after the game concluded, my phone rang, and I knew it wasn't good news. The nurse said, "I'm very sorry, John, your dad just passed away." The only thing I could think to say was, "See, I told you my dad was watching the game."

I'm convinced my mom was calling out to him from the other side, urging, "Come on, Harold, hurry up and join me. I want to go somewhere."

At that moment, I realized I had become an orphan.

They truly were the best parents a son could ever wish for.

ACT 18

To Catch a Thief

"In a mystery, the sleuth must be believably involved and emotionally invested in solving the crime."
- Diane Mott Davidson -

A couple of years back, my car got broken into while parked in my driveway. The thief took a bag containing two old Macintosh laptops, which I used as loaners for clients during repairs. Although the laptops were valued at around $1000 combined, they were quite outdated, so the loss wasn't significant. I reported the incident to the police, but their hopes of recovering the laptops were slim.

About a month later, while providing remote support for a client, I noticed something unusual. A special software I used to connect and troubleshoot with clients remotely displayed one of the stolen laptops as online. I accessed the laptop and shared the screen. It turned out the computer was being used to browse a specific Facebook page. I observed as the user, named Angel, typed in Spanish. Luckily, my high school Spanish classes came in handy. I managed to find Angel's public profile, and in my excitement, I shared the unbelievable news on my own Facebook page.

After Angel logged off, I delved into his Facebook profile for clues to his identity and location. I meticulously documented any information that could aid in recovering the laptop and catching the thief. I stumbled upon Angel's full name, a picture of him, and another image of him next to a recently purchased used car, complete with a visible license plate – a stroke of luck indeed!

The next day, I contacted the police detective assigned to my case and provided him with all the details I had gathered. Despite his limited technical knowledge, we arranged to meet at the station on Monday for a review of everything I had gathered.

Later on, my app alerted me that the stolen laptop was online again. This time, I managed to acquire more data, such as the Wi-Fi network name, password and a 10-digit telephone number that seemed to belong to the place where Angel was staying. Although I couldn't pinpoint the laptop's location using my software, I discovered the Prey project, a tool that not only tracked the laptop's whereabouts but also captured snapshots from its webcam. The challenge now lay in finding a way to install this software on my stolen laptop.

The following day, I discovered that he had been online earlier in the evening. Upon returning home, I discreetly uploaded the Prey Project installer to my laptop. Installing the software required remote access, so I seized the opportunity when the mouse movements ceased. Assuming he had stepped away, I proceeded to install the Prey software swiftly. Although Angel noticed unusual mouse movements and window activities and promptly shut down the laptop, he later restarted it, inadvertently completing the software installation.

Soon after, I began receiving location reports through local Wi-Fi, providing accurate details. Additionally, the software started sending me snapshots from the laptop's camera, allowing me to see the individual using the device. The images matched Angel's Facebook profile, and Google Maps pin pointed the laptop's exact location.

The next day, I visited the police station with evidence in hand. The detective was intrigued by how I acquired such information, to which I reminded him of my I.T. expertise. With ample evidence, the detective decided to take action. He informed me that he would visit the address associated with the laptop that evening.

Following his visit, the detective reported back the next day, sharing that he had approached the house in question. A woman answered the door and denied knowing Angel upon seeing his photo. However, her son later called the detective, admitting that Angel resided in a separate dwelling behind the house. Unfortunately, Angel had fled upon seeing the detectives at the front door, leaving the detective's efforts unrewarded.

Picture courtesy of Prey Project

After three weeks offline, my laptop, and my hopes, seemed lost in the digital abyss. Despite this setback, I maintained an active online presence, documenting every step of the investigation on Facebook, attracting a devoted audience that likened it to gripping crime dramas on TV. The thrill of the chase was dampened by the laptop's absence from cyberspace.

A glimmer of hope appeared as the laptop came back online, revealing a new location through the Prey software. The triangulation led us to a cluster of houses in close proximity. Armed with cameras and gadgets, my friend Gary and I embarked on a reconnaissance mission in South Los Angeles. After a bit of sleuthing, we pinpointed the matching house and noted the address.

Upon returning, I shared the newfound address with the detective, offering a fresh lead to apprehend the culprit. Despite his puzzlement at my investigative prowess, the detective, accompanied by his Spanish-speaking partner, planned to pay a visit. Wary of tipping off the suspect, I proposed a different approach to ensure a successful capture. The detective's supervisor overheard our conversation, amused by my unconventional suggestion and endorsed the plan, eager to see how the events would unfold.

The following evening, I eagerly waited at my desk, eyes fixed on the computer screen, hoping for a sign that Angel was online once more. The detective called, mentioning his proximity to Angel's location, and advising me to contact him when Angel reappeared online. Unfortunately, Angel did not log on that evening, leaving me disappointed. Upon informing the detective that Angel seemed absent, he humorously remarked, "Welcome to police work," and agreed to attempt again the next day. On the subsequent evening, I had dinner plans with close friends, so I arrived early at their place and requested the use of their computer to monitor the situation.

Intrigued, my friends joined me around the screen as we awaited Angel's online presence. Suddenly, Angel was back online. I swiftly informed the detective, who, though delayed, assured me of his imminent arrival. Utilizing the Prey software, I prepared to activate a siren sound from the computer speakers, providing probable cause for the detective to enter the premises and apprehend Angel.

As we awaited the detective's call, minutes passed without any news. Curiosity led me to take snapshots using the laptop camera. To my amazement, the images revealed law enforcement entering through the front door, arresting Angel, and placing him in handcuffs. The thief was caught!

Picture courtesy of my Laptop Camera

Shortly after, the detective confirmed the successful recovery of the laptop and Angel's arrest. I recounted witnessing the events in real-time. The detective explained how they found Angel with the laptop on his lap upon their arrival, prompting him to flee to the back door. Fortunately, officers stationed at the rear of the house intercepted Angel as he tried to escape, bringing him back inside. The laptop's positioning on the couch allowed me to capture the moment of the arrest.

The detective expressed his gratitude and informed me that I could retrieve my laptop the following day, as it was no longer needed as evidence due to the information I had provided. Although the adventure spanned nearly four months, the outcome was truly rewarding. Friends fondly recall the story, reminiscing about the excitement of following the events unfolded on Facebook.

Picture with Leo Stallworth courtesy of Channel 7, Eyewitness News

Pearls of Wisdom
Foster a Positive Mindset

Cultivating a positive mindset can significantly impact how we confront challenges. Encourage others to concentrate on aspects they can influence and to seek the silver lining in difficult circumstances.

I often share the Serenity Prayer

"Lord, grant me the serenity to accept the things I cannot change, the courage to change the things I can, and the wisdom to know the difference."

Establish Small Goals

When encountering a major challenge, breaking it down into smaller, manageable objectives can be beneficial. Encourage others to set realistic goals and celebrate their achievements along the way. This approach helps build confidence and provide a sense of accomplishment.

Provide Support

Sometimes, a little support is all someone needs. Be present for others during tough times. Listen to their concerns, offer words of encouragement, and remind them of their strengths. Knowing that someone believes in them can inspire individuals to continue moving forward.

Highlight Strengths and Achievements

Encourage others to acknowledge their strengths and past successes. Remind them of moments when they overcame obstacles. This can enhance their confidence and reinforce their capability to succeed once more.

Promote Self-Care

Self-care is essential during challenging times. Urge others to prioritize their well-being by ensuring they get adequate rest, eat nutritious meals, and participate in activities they love. When individuals feel good both physically and emotionally, they are more prepared to tackle difficulties.

Create a Positive Environment

Being surrounded by uplifting individuals can significantly impact one's outlook. Foster a supportive community where everyone encourages each other. A positive atmosphere can elevate spirits and motivate action. Sometimes, a simple act of kindness can assist someone in their time of need.

Teach Resilience

Resilience is the capacity to recover from setbacks. Guide others in understanding that experiencing failure is acceptable and a natural part of the journey. Inspire them to learn from their errors and continue progressing forward.

Encourage Action

Taking action often serves as a powerful motivator. Inspire others to make small strides toward their goals, regardless of how overwhelming the challenge may appear. Each step taken fosters momentum and builds confidence.

Celebrate Successes

Recognizing achievements, no matter how minor, is crucial. Acknowledge and celebrate each victory along the journey. This practice reinforces the notion that progress is occurring and helps maintain high levels of motivation.

With encouragement and resolve, anyone can rise above challenges and fulfill their aspirations, regardless of their nature.

ACT 19

---◆---

Yet Another Challenge to Overcome

"The reasonable man adapts himself to the world; the unreasonable one persists to adapt the world to himself. Therefore all progress depends on the unreasonable man."
- George Bernard Shaw -

My life was progressing quite well. Business was stable. I was receiving a few speaking engagements, and I performed magic several nights a week. Overall, I was happy.

I embarked on my annual poker cruise, this time heading to the Caribbean. Playing poker with friends on Card Player Cruises was always a getaway I eagerly anticipated. Jan, Linda, Mark and Tina, who manage the cruise company, have become dear friends, along with several staff members and dealers. I believe this was my 24th cruise with the group.

As I disembarked from the ship at the end of February 2020, I began hearing reports about a mysterious flu spreading from Asia. Little did I realize that life as we knew it was about to change dramatically.

Covid-19 quickly became the focal point of nearly every conversation. People began to fall ill, and some sadly lost their lives. By mid-March, we were advised to stay home, no exceptions.

I had put in a tremendous effort to accept my facial paralysis and no longer felt the need to shy away from social events or avoid being photographed. However, with the pandemic, wearing a mask became not just a social norm but a government requirement.

By this point in my life, I had spent twenty years learning to celebrate my facial difference and developing my core motivational speaking message that "Being Different is Your Superpower."

I was not about to let this pandemic derail my newfound life's mission.

As a proud member of the tight-knit community of individuals with cranio-facial differences, I sought ways to celebrate my facial paralysis once more. I discovered a company online that created custom Covid masks. After uploading a picture of my face from the nose down, I received a few cloth masks featuring an image of my paralyzed face.

On the rare occasion I ventured outside, I noticed that strangers would cast a quick glance at my new mask and continue on their way. However, when I encountered someone familiar, they would pause and do a double take. I could see in their eyes that they grasped the message I was conveying: I was consciously choosing not to hide my face, even amidst a global pandemic.

PEARLS OF WISDOM
The Importance of a Smile

William Shakespeare once wrote, "A smile cures the wounding of a frown," and some scientists suggest that it takes only seventeen muscles to smile, whereas frowning requires forty three.

In this section, I want to highlight something often overlooked, yet profoundly impactful: the power of a smile.

A smile is a simple yet potent gesture that can significantly influence those around us. It is a universal expression that crosses borders, cultures, and languages. A smile can make others feel acknowledged, valued, and appreciated. It has the ability to brighten someone's day and help them momentarily set aside their worries.

So, why don't we share smiles more frequently?

Moreover, smiling positively affects our own lives as well. When we smile, our brains release endorphins, which act as natural pain relievers and mood enhancers. This simple act can lower stress and bolster our immune system. Additionally, smiling makes us appear more attractive, approachable, and confident.

As Bob Marley eloquently stated, "The most beautiful curve on a woman's body is her smile."

Through my long journey of self-acceptance and love, people began to see the real me. They were willing to look beyond my face, allowing friendships to bloom again, despite my imperfect smile.

Practicing magic and sharing my stories to inspire others has rekindled joy in my life. I discovered that my friends cherished me for my heart and character, not my appearance.

Roy T. Bennett said that "A smile puts you on the right track. A smile makes the world a beautiful place. When you lose your smile, you lose your way in the chaos of life."

I started viewing my scars as hard-earned badges of honor. I learned to transform my struggles into messages of hope, and you can too, inspiring others along the way.

My experiences have taught me the profound impact of a simple smile; it can ease tension and foster trust. Yet, despite these advantages, we often overlook the power of a smile, don't we? How much time and effort does it truly require?

We frequently become entangled in our daily routines, challenges, and worries, forgetting to pause and express gratitude to those around us and to the positive aspects of our lives.

Smiling helps diminish our insecurities and fears by inviting others to accept, and perhaps even love us. This connection with others is my secret to happiness.

I encourage you all to smile more frequently. Share your smile with loved ones, colleagues, neighbors, and even strangers on the street. You never know just how much your smile may brighten someone else's day.

Rolodex Roulette

During the Covid-19 shutdown, I found myself spending a significant amount of time at home. I've always been the kind of person who prefers calling friends on their birthdays rather than sending a text or posting a generic message on their Facebook profiles.

This is when I came up with a fun idea for a game that I call *Rolodex Roulette*. For those unfamiliar with a rolodex, it was a spindle that held numerous cards containing contacts and their information, organized alphabetically for easy access to phone numbers or addresses. Nowadays, rolodexes have been replaced by the contact lists in our phones and computers.

I would open my contact list on my phone and scroll randomly until I landed on a name. It didn't matter whether I had spoken to them recently or if it had been years. I would call just to say hello and check in. Since most people were at home during that time, they were likely to answer the phone. Often, conversations with those I hadn't spoken to in years would begin with, "Hello, John?"

I would quickly say hi and explain my new game intended to foster connections. Many times, these conversations would lead to fond reminiscing about good times and shared memories. By the end of the calls, numerous friends would say, "That was fun! I'm going to start playing your game!"

That was my exact intention.

Another advantage of this game was that it provided plausible deniability when reaching out to someone with whom I had a disagreement or falling out. Many people hesitate to be the first to mend a strained relationship. This game allowed me to simply say that the rules required me to call a randomly chosen person.

It's amusing how effectively this disarmed the other person, and before long, we were laughing about how a trivial issue, which we hardly remembered, had damaged our friendship.

Inside the

Magician's Studio

Being confined at home for days on end left me longing for the company of my friends from The Magic Castle. For nearly ten years, my Friday routine had revolved around visiting the Castle for a casual buffet lunch followed by a magic show in the Close-up Gallery. After a while, I began to see the same familiar faces week after week. I was welcomed to join my friends Ruthie and Darryl Payne, Fred and Helen Lack and a few others at a cozy round table each Friday.

This group of friends became my new family after the passing of both my parents a few years prior. We grew close, and I affectionately referred to Ruthie and Darryl as Mom and Dad. It was during this time that I truly understood how the sudden loss of my parents was impacting me. Becoming their faux stepson became incredibly significant for all of us; it was an extraordinary gift.

The Castle was closed for nearly two years, and I found myself cut off from my new family, missing our weekly lunches, not to mention my regular dose of incredible magic.

Darryl, Ruthie, Yours Truly, Helen & Fred

One day, as I was admitedly feeling lonely and sorry for myself, I had a crazy idea! With Zoom becoming an essential tool for safe, face-to-face meetings, (no pun intended,) I decided to host a virtual Friday lunch every week. I would invite friends from The Castle who I could no longer see in person.

Each week, I would select a magician friend and kindly ask them to perform some virtual magic. As the pandemic had put a damper on live entertainment, magicians had to adapt and start performing online to earn their living.

I named the event "Inside the Magician's Studio," inspired by the PBS show "Inside the Actors Studio." The format consisted of a 30-minute meet and greet with friends from the Castle, followed by a 20-minute magic performance, and then a 20-30 minute interview segment. My goal was for the audience to not only enjoy the magic but also learn about the performer and their choice of magic as a means of self-expression.

My ambition for the show was to feature a different magician each week. I began by inviting friends from the Castle to perform. Before I knew it, the word spread like wildfire throughout the magic community. Soon, I was receiving inquiries from some of the most renowned and respected magicians worldwide, eager to be a guest star.

Initially, I worried that I might run out of talented magicians as the pandemic began to ease. To my surprise, I surpassed my initial goal of showcasing 52 magicians, one each week without any repeats. I discovered incredible magicians from distant lands who were excited to accept my invitation to perform.

One of my most memorable guests, Javi Benetiz, confided in me that he didn't have a professional Zoom setup and was worried about the technical aspects. I reassured him that my audience was very understanding and would not let any tech issues detract from their enjoyment of his performance. A few weeks later, Javi agreed to appear on the show. Despite some technical hiccups, the show turned out to be fantastic.

A couple weeks later, Javi reached out to me privately. He expressed his genuine concern about how he would manage financially, since all his live performances had been canceled for the foreseeable future.

With heartfelt gratitude, he thanked me, saying that without my encouragement to try performing on a virtual stage, he would have had to abandon his magic career and seek alternative income.

Javi also shared that he was able to offer many clients who had canceled, an opportunity to still experience his incredible magic. Remarkably, he even mentioned that his income increased since he no longer had the costs associated with traveling from city to city to perform.

The show continued to thrive as word spread. A group of magicians from Aaron Fisher's Conjuring Community became a valuable source of talent. I invited Jack, the entertainment director of The Castle, to attend my free weekly show. An incredible transformation began to unfold. Jack now had access to a new pool of exceptional magicians to add to his talent roster. I believe ten of my guests received invitations to perform in the Castle's Saturday evening virtual show, and once the Castle reopened, five of them were hired to perform in the Close-up Gallery.

It was a tremendous honor to facilitate these connections and help these magicians realize one of their lifelong dreams.

At the time of writing this book, I have hosted a total of 220 of the world's most respected magicians and counting. I must admit, this has selfishly brought me some recognition within the global community of professional magicians, many of whom have become close personal friends. I hope to keep offering this show weekly to the world until I either run out of remarkable magicians or magic enthusiasts willing to attend.

This is yet another way how I've discovered to give back to the art of magic, which has generously contributed to restoring my self-respect and rediscovering true joy in my life.

I would always conclude each episode by asking, "What is your definition of magic?"

My own definition evolved over time, ultimately becoming, "Magic is the feeling you experience when your eyes and senses encounter something your brain cannot comprehend." Many of my guests' definitions were recorded and shared on my website.

I was eager to discover if there was a common theme among the definitions. Indeed, there was: Magic exists in the minds and hearts of the spectators.

> *"Magic is believing in yourself. If you can make that happen, you can make anything happen."*
> *– Goethe –*

ACT 20

Triumph Over Adversity

" I now see how owning our story and loving ourselves through that process is the bravest thing that we will ever do."
- Brené Brown -

My journey of overcoming challenges has taught me the importance of sharing the skills and insights I've gained, which is why I decided to become a motivational speaker.

Learning to thrive after a life-changing event is essential for survival. Life can shift in an instant—sometimes bringing exciting opportunities, such as starting a new job or relocating to a new city, while other times presenting significant challenges, like the loss of a loved one or confronting a serious health issue. Regardless of the nature of the change, it is possible to flourish and rediscover happiness. This section outlines steps you can take to promote growth and progress following a transformative event.

The first step is to, *embrace your emotions*. When a significant event occurs, feeling a range of emotions is completely normal. You may experience sadness, anger, confusion, or even relief. Accepting these feelings is crucial. Avoid judging yourself for what you feel; instead, allow yourself to fully experience these emotions, as they are an inherent part of being human.

Healing is a gradual process that varies for each person, so don't rush. Permit yourself the time you need to process what has occurred. This may involve taking a break from work or spending time alone to reflect. During this time, be kind and gentle with yourself.

You don't have to face this journey alone. Reach out to friends or family to share your feelings—expressing your thoughts can lighten your emotional burden. Additionally, consider joining support groups where you can connect with others who have experienced similar challenges. Knowing that you are not alone can provide immense comfort.

After a significant change, it's beneficial to contemplate your aspirations for the future. Establishing new goals gives you something positive to look forward to. Start with small, attainable objectives. For instance, if you aim to enhance your health, you might commit to walking for just 10 minutes each day. As you accomplish these little goals, you'll gain the confidence to tackle larger ones.

Self-care is crucial during difficult periods. Ensure that you nourish your body with healthy food, maintain a proper sleep schedule, and engage in regular exercise. Dedicate time to activities you enjoy, such as reading, painting, or spending time outdoors. Prioritizing self-care can help you feel more balanced and uplift your mood.

Sometimes, a significant life event can spark personal growth or new insights. Try to discover meaning in your experiences. Reflect on what you have learned about yourself or identify changes you wish to make in your life. This introspection can guide you forward with a fresh perspective.

While embracing change can be daunting, it can also unveil new opportunities. Be open to exploring new paths and experiences. Often, the most rewarding aspects of life arise from unexpected changes. Stay curious and open-minded as you adapt to your new circumstances.

"The meaning of life is to find your gift. The purpose of life is to give it away."
- Pablo Picasso -

Finally, concentrating on what you're grateful for can shift your mindset positively. Create a list of things, both big and small, that bring you joy—this could range from a cozy cup of coffee to the warmth of a kind friend or the beauty of a sunny day. Practicing gratitude can help you uncover happiness, even during challenging times.

Recovering and thriving after a life-altering event is achievable, even if it feels daunting initially. By embracing your emotions, allowing yourself time to heal, seeking support, establishing new goals, prioritizing self-care, discovering new meaning, remaining open to change, and cultivating gratitude, you can reconstruct your life. Keep in mind that while life may have changed, it can still be rich and joyful. You possess the strength to move ahead and flourish.

Fear
is a
Double Edged
Sword

Another topic I frequently discuss is the idea of fear as a double-edged sword.

Fear is an emotion that everyone faces. It can evoke feelings of fright, worry, or anxiety. However, fear isn't solely negative; it can also serve a beneficial purpose. This section will delve into how fear acts like a double-edged sword, capable of both assisting and hindering us simultaneously.

Understanding that fear is our body's protective mechanism is crucial. When we experience fear, our brain sends signals meant to safeguard us. For instance, encountering a snake can trigger a fear response that prompts us to leap back quickly. This reaction is known as the "fight or flight" response, preparing our bodies to confront the threat or escape from it.

Fear Has a Positive Side

Fear can serve as a powerful motivator. When we dread failing at a job interview, it often prompts us to prepare more diligently, which can enhance our performance and increase our chances for success.

Fear also encourages caution. It can prevent us from making reckless choices. For instance, the fear of injury may deter us from taking unnecessary risks, such as climbing a tall tree without proper safety measures.

Confronting our fears can foster personal growth. By facing what frightens us, we often emerge stronger. For example, someone who has a fear of public speaking can enhance their abilities through practice and by performing in front of a smaller audience.

On the flip side, fear can sometimes hinder us from pursuing our desires or necessities. If someone is overly afraid to embrace new experiences, they might miss valuable opportunities. An example is the fear of flying, which could stop someone from exploring new destinations.

Persistent fear can lead to anxiety, a nagging feeling of worry that lingers. This can disrupt our daily lives, making it challenging to focus or enjoy activities we once cherished.

When we allow fear to dominate our lives, we may shy away from situations that could promote our growth. This can result in a smaller, more restricted existence. For instance, someone who is anxious about meeting new people might miss out on forming new friendships.

"I learned that courage was not the absence of fear, but the triumph over it. The brave man is not he who does not feel afraid, but he who conquers that fear."
- Nelson Mandela -

The Key to Navigating Fear: Finding Balance

The first step to achieving balance is identifying your fears. Take a moment to write down what frightens you. Gaining clarity on your fears can enhance your understanding of them.

Next, challenge your fears. It's essential to Ask yourself whether your fear stems from facts or mere assumptions. Often, our fears appear larger in our minds than they are in reality.

Additionally, practice self-compassion. It's perfectly normal to feel afraid. Treat yourself with kindness as you face your fears. Remember, fear is a universal experience; it is part of being human.

Fear has a dual nature. While it can serve as a protective force and a source of motivation, it can also hinder us. By comprehending our fears and discovering ways to confront them, we can leverage fear to our advantage. Rather than allowing fear to dictate our lives, we can learn to embrace it, grow from it, and move forward. Ultimately, it's not about eradicating fear but mastering it and transforming it into a tool for personal growth.

"Nothing in life is to be feared, it is only to be understood. Now is the time to understand more, so that we may fear less."
- Marie Curie -

"Feed Your Heart with Your Art"

My signature keynote is titled "Feed Your Heart with Your Art." Art serves as a profound means of self-expression, encompassing activities like painting, drawing, writing, dancing, or any creative endeavor that brings us joy.

In this section, we will delve into how the act of creating art can nourish our hearts, fostering greater happiness and a deeper connection with ourselves and those around us.

Art is not solely about crafting something visually appealing; it is about conveying what lies within us. Through creation, we communicate our thoughts and emotions, often expressing feelings that may be difficult to articulate verbally. For instance, if you're feeling down, drawing or painting can serve as a unique outlet to express that sadness. Personally, my chosen art form is close-up magic.

Engaging in artistic activities can infuse our lives with joy. When we immerse ourselves in the creative process, we enter a state of flow, losing track of time and becoming fully absorbed in our work. Whether it's blending paints to achieve the ideal shade or crafting a narrative, the act of creation can elevate our spirits and fill our hearts with happiness.

Art can be a potent healing mechanism, as illustrated by my previous stories of Ron, Daryn and Alex. During challenging times, creating art can aid in processing our emotions.

For example, someone grieving the loss of a loved one may find solace in writing a poem or assembling a memory scrapbook. Art allows us to navigate our feelings and discover tranquility amidst life's hardships.

Sharing your art with others, especially when it comes from the heart, can deepen connections and uplift those around you. By showcasing your work, you welcome others into your world, which can foster conversations and friendships. Whether it's exhibiting your paintings at a local café or sharing your writing with friends, expressing your creativity can cultivate a sense of community and support.

Amid our busy lives, it's essential to carve out time for art. Dedicate a few minutes each day or week to focus on your creative endeavors. This might be as simple as doodling in a notebook or journaling. By prioritizing art, you nourish your heart and nurture your soul.

Keep in mind that art doesn't need to be flawless. The act of creating holds more significance than the final outcome. Allow yourself the freedom to make mistakes and explore new ideas. Embracing imperfection can relieve pressure and enhance the joy of creation.

Finally, your art serves as a reflection of your identity. It narrates your story, experiences, and aspirations. Take the time to reflect on what you wish to convey through your creations. What themes or messages resonate with you? By clarifying what you want to express, you can produce more meaningful works that truly resonate with your heart.

"Living is the art of loving. Loving is the art of caring.
Caring is the art of sharing. Sharing is the art of living.
If you want to lift yourself up, lift up someone else."
- Booker T. Washington -

Connecting with yourself and others through your art is a truly beautiful experience. Art brings joy, healing, expression, and in my case, the performance of magic, enriching your life in countless ways. Set aside time to create, seek inspiration, and cherish the journey of artistic expression. Keep in mind that it's not solely about the final product; it's about the emotions and experiences you gather throughout the process. Allow your art to feed your heart and soul, and witness the transformative power it can have on your life.

My joy is in sharing the wonder and awe with the audience.

Picture courtesy of Taylor Wong - Magic Castle Photographer

"Never forget that you are one of a kind. Never forget that if there weren't any need for you, in all your uniqueness, to be on this earth, you wouldn't be here in the first place. And never forget, no matter how overwhelming life's challenges and problems seem to be, that one person can make a difference in the world. In fact, it is always because of one person that all the changes that matter in the world come about. So be that one person."
– R. Buckminster Fuller –

ACT 21

Performing Magic is a Way of Life

"Whatever you do in life, if you want to be creative and intelligent, and develop your brain, you must do everything with the awareness that everything, in some way, connects to everything else."
- Leonardo Da Vinci -

As a magician, I always carry a few tricks up my sleeve, ready to perform whenever the moment strikes. You never know when you might be able to lighten a tense situation with a bit of magic.

One day, I answered a knock at my door from a real estate agent. He mentioned that a developer was interested in purchasing my home. I had considered selling and was aware of the housing prices in my neighborhood. When the agent asked if I was interested, I jokingly replied, "If the price is right, call me Bob Barker." The agent looked puzzled and asked, "Bob who?" I chuckled, realizing he was probably younger than I assumed. I decided to throw out an outrageous figure – roughly half a million more than I believed my house was worth. To my surprise, the agent agreed, saying that it was the maximum amount he was allowed to offer.

I requested the weekend to think it over, and he consented. I insisted that the sale contract include a contingency for me to find a new home, along with a two-month period to move after closing the deal. The developer accepted my conditions, and it was time to begin the house-hunting process. I chose to work with his real estate agent, which would save me an extra 2%.

My previous home was conveniently located near Ventura Boulevard, the main thoroughfare in the San Fernando valley, and I was open to moving a bit further north for a larger house on a bigger lot at a better price.

Every Saturday, we would visit open houses, and I hated each one of them. I was searching for a property on a large lot with an open floor plan, but my hopes were beginning to fade. I had to expand my search beyond my preferred area. One day, he texted me an address of a listed house, and we decided to meet there first thing Saturday morning.

We arrived just as che owners were about to leave. I introduced myself and performed a little magic for the owner, and her daughter. It turned out that she was a theater teacher at a nearby junior college. I mentioned that I had graduated from Cal State Northridge with a degree in theater. After they both left, my realtor and I stepped inside.

To my surprise, the living room and kitchen showcased a spacious open floor plan. The garage had been transformed into a vast room that would be perfect for an indoor movie theater. One of the other bedrooms had been converted into an office, and there were three additional bedrooms. Finally, I would have one or two spare bedrooms for guests!

I stepped into the backyard and was instantly captivated by two magnificent ash trees towering at 60 feet. Their expansive canopy provided ample shade. Nearby, I noticed a detached three-car garage with a patio cover, and I could easily envision transforming this space into a performance area where an audience could enjoy my magic show.

I had discovered the home of my dreams, and the best part was that it was located in a cul-de-sac, occupying the largest pie-shaped lot in the neighborhood.

My realtor and I returned to my house and quickly drafted an offer. Remarkably, the price was nearly six hundred thousand dollars less than what I had been offered for my previous home. Along with my offer, I included a letter with my offer, sharing my love for her house and my vision for converting the garage into a dedicated theater for magic performances.

The Winnetka Mystery Theatre of Wizardry

Two weeks later, I received a call from my well-known magician friend, Paul Gertner. He inquired about my connection to the owner, and I asked him how he knew her. He revealed that they were related and that she had reached out to him to ask if he knew a magician named Kippen. Paul immediately affirmed this, and when she mentioned I was interested in purchasing her house, he wholeheartedly endorsed me. The next day, she accepted my offer.

It was time to sign the loan documents, which coincided with the peak of the pandemic. The notary I had hired, knocked on the door. Peeping through the peephole, I saw her double-masked and gloved. Since I had received all my vaccinations, I felt at ease inviting her in. We sat at my kitchen table, sifting through the numerous loan documents. She struggled to moisten her thumb to turn the pages quickly, inadvertently touching her mask each time. We both chuckled at this habitual quirk. We connected well and shared a similar sense of humor.

Once we finished signing the documents, she took one last look around and said, "Alright, John, I believe we're done." I replied, "You may be finished, but I'm definitely not done." Her expression shifted to one of concern. I smiled and explained that she was the first stranger I'd encountered in months, and I felt the urge to perform some magic for her. She chuckled, saying, "Alright, let me make a quick call first." She contacted her next client, and I caught her side of the conversation.

"Hi Pete. No, I'm still on my way... I'm just running a little late. No, no... everything's fine. Umm, I'm being held hostage by a magician who insists that I be his audience." They both laughed before she hung up.

I proceeded to perform about ten minutes of close-up magic. It was a delightful experience for her and a huge relief for me, as it had been months since I last performed. Magic truly has a way of making everything come together.

It was now time for a shopping trip. I needed to buy some new furniture for both the living room and the indoor theater.

My friend Gary and I decided to visit a local La-Z-Boy furniture store. As we walked in, we were greeted by a young saleswoman wearing a COVID mask. She asked if we needed assistance, and I replied that we would let her know if we had any questions.

We made our way to the sectional area. With a picture of the new entertainment room in hand, we tried to envision how this large sectional couch would fit. The saleswoman approached us and offered to send a lovely associate with a tape measure to my new house. She could create a furniture plan to ensure everything would fit perfectly. I explained that I didn't have access to the new house yet and didn't want to disturb the owner, who was packing for the move. However, I wanted to arrange for delivery the week after closing.

Next, we moved to the leather furniture section. There, we discovered a comfortable couch, loveseat, and recliner. We settled down to test the comfort, and it was incredibly cozy. Once again, the saleswoman came over and reminded me that without her associate measuring the room, I would be unable to return the furniture. I thanked her but reiterated that I had heard her the first time.

It was Labor Day weekend, and the store was promoting significant sales. I inquired with the saleslady about the total cost of three pieces of furniture. She informed me it would be just under eight thousand dollars. Ouch! I hadn't anticipated spending that much on just three items. As I settled into the comfortable recliner, aware that I was making a significant profit from selling my house, I found myself saying, "Okay, when could they be delivered?" She replied, "Oh, I haven't even checked if they're in stock." My frustration began to rise. I asked her to please verify.

After about ten minutes, she returned with disappointing news: two of the three pieces were out of stock. I then asked when I might receive them, and she said it would take around six months. My irritation grew. I had clearly stated my timeline, and it felt completely overlooked. For those who don't know me, when I get annoyed, I tend to raise my voice—a skill honed from my theater training, ensuring even those in the back row can hear me.

Just then, another employee stepped in to assist. Interestingly, she turned out to be the kind lady who would go out to measure.

She pointed out the furniture I selected was the electric version, complete with motors and remote controls. I remarked that it seemed excessive and inquired about the price of the non-motorized options. She informed me they were not only $2,600 cheaper but that all three pieces were in stock. I agreed right away.

I stood up and walked over to the counter, credit card in hand. At that moment, the manager approached from the back of the store, asking what all the commotion was about. I apologized, explaining that I had gotten a bit worked up, but everything was fine now.

To lighten the atmosphere, I decided to perform a magic trick. I pulled out four cards from my pocket: two fives and two kings, each from different suits. I asked the manager, to extend her hand, and I placed the two fives face down in her palm while showing that I was holding the kings.

Once the cards were face down, I asked her to remember which cards were which. She confidently stated she had the two fives, while I held the two kings. With a snap of my fingers, I slowly revealed that I now held the fives, and she was left with the kings.

She exclaimed, "Oh my God, how did you do that?" She then shared her love for playing cards and mentioned that she played poker weekly. This sparked a clever idea in my mind. I asked Gary to head to the car and retrieve a full deck from the center console.

As Gary returned, I shuffled the cards while asking Jan if she had a favorite card. She replied, "Absolutely! It's the 3 of diamonds." Curious, I asked if she was feeling lucky today, and she smiled in response.

I then proposed a little game: I would fan the cards face down, and if she randomly selected her favorite, the 3 of diamonds, I would receive an additional ten percent off the furniture price. She eagerly accepted, saying, "I'm game, let's gamble."

I fanned out the cards, and she picked one, immediately holding it against her chest without looking. Turning to the lady at the register, I inquired about applying the extra ten percent discount. Jan suddenly paused and said, "Wait, I haven't even looked at the card I chose." I playfully reminded her that time was ticking. With her head tilted down, she slowly glanced at the card. To her astonishment, she revealed it was indeed her favorite. I reassured her that I was a skilled magician, not a hustler attempting to take advantage of her.

She agreed to the additional discount. Handing her the deck, I asked her to shuffle the cards. As a seasoned poker player, she shuffled with enthusiasm.

After five or six thorough mixes, I asked her how much the sales tax would be. She mentioned around six hundred dollars. I then suggested we try one more time: if she picked her favorite card again from the face down, fanned-out deck, she would discount the sales tax.

She chuckled, saying, "That's impossible! I just shuffled the cards six times, and you haven't even looked at them!" Still, she reached in and pulled out another card. To her surprise and disbelief, it was once again the 3 of diamonds. She hugged me tightly as we left the store.

The lesson? Never gamble with a professional magician.

"The art of a magician is to create wonder. If we live with a sense of wonder, our lives become filled with joy."
– Doug Henning –

PEARLS OF WISDOM
Discovering Magic in the Wild

Magic is often associated with spells, wands, and mythical creatures. However, it also resides in our daily lives. It's about discovering the enchantment in the mundane and cherishing the little things that bring us joy. Here are some ways to uncover magic in your everyday routine.

Wonders of Nature

One of the simplest places to find magic is in the natural world. Admire a stunning flower, observe the clouds morphing shapes, or listen to the soothing sound of rain. Nature reminds us of the incredible beauty surrounding us. Take a moment to step outside, inhale the fresh air, and appreciate the wonders around you.

Acts of Kindness

Magic often emerges through acts of kindness. A friendly smile from a stranger, a heartfelt compliment from a friend, or lending a helping hand to someone in need can create a truly magical atmosphere. These small gestures enhance our world and remind us of the inherent goodness in others.

The Magic of Imagination

Imagination itself is a form of magic. When you daydream or weave stories in your mind, you access a world full of possibilities. You can transform into anything and travel anywhere. Nurture your imagination by reading books, drawing, or engaging in creative games that inspire you.

Cherished Everyday Moments

Sometimes, magic lies within the simplest moments. This might involve sharing a meal with loved ones, witnessing a breathtaking sunset, or listening to your favorite song. Take the time to notice and relish these moments—they serve as magical reminders of what truly matters in life.

Embracing New Experiences

Uncovering something new can feel truly enchanting. Whether it's acquiring a new skill, experimenting with a fresh recipe, or delving into a new hobby, the thrill of learning unlocks a world of possibilities. Embrace the joy of discovery and allow it to fuel your inspiration.

Mindfulness and Being Present

Engaging in mindfulness enables you to fully appreciate the here and now. By being completely present in your current activities, you can find wonder in even the most mundane tasks, such as doing dishes or enjoying a shower. Pay attention to the sensations, sounds, and feelings that accompany these moments.

Cultivating Gratitude

Taking a moment to reflect on what you're thankful for can infuse your life with a sense of magic. Consider jotting down a few things each day that bring you joy. This practice shifts your focus toward the positive elements in life and can transform ordinary days into something extraordinary.

Fostering Connections with Others

Nurturing relationships with friends and family creates a magical bond. Share stories, enjoy laughter, and provide support for one another. These connections enrich our lives and add a touch of magic to our everyday interactions.

Embrace the Everyday

Discover joy in the mundane. Celebrate minor victories, such as completing a project, navigating a hectic day, or simply relishing a cup of tea. Acknowledging the wonder in the ordinary enriches our lives and brings a sense of fulfillment.

"There is no insurmountable solitude. All paths lead to the same goal: to convey to others what we are. And we must pass through solitude and difficulty, isolation and silence in order to reach forth to the enchanted place where we can dance our clumsy dance and sing our sorrowful song - but in this dance or in this song there are fulfilled the most ancient rites of our conscience in the awareness of being human and of believing in a common destiny."
- Pablo Neruda -

ACT 22

Life Coaching

" Coaching is unlocking a person's potential to maximize their own performance. It is helping them to learn rather than teaching them."
- Timothy Gallwey -

As I continue to seek out more speaking opportunities, I find I can equally help and inspire others through my life coaching practice. I now assist clients around the world through platforms like Zoom and Google Meet.

In my role as a life coach, I empower clients to set and achieve their goals while enriching their lives. Below is my core coaching framework:

Discovering Clarity and Focus

I guide my clients in uncovering their genuine desires. Together, we pinpoint their goals and priorities, providing clarity on what to concentrate on and the order in which to tackle them.

Accountability

I find that keeping my clients accountable proves to be highly advantageous. I regularly check on their progress and inspire them to stay committed to their objectives.

Custom Guidance Through Thought-Provoking Questions

My skill in asking insightful questions helps clients identify their limiting beliefs. I then provide constructive feedback to aid them in crafting a master plan tailored to their unique needs.

Support and Encouragement

As a life coach, I offer unwavering support and encouragement during tough times. Together, we celebrate victories over challenges, which helps to elevate my clients' confidence.

Enhanced Decision-Making

I guide my clients in making well-informed decisions by presenting diverse perspectives. Through thought-provoking questions, I encourage them to engage in deep reflection about their choices.

Skills Development

Working alongside my clients, I help them to develop essential skills such as time management, communication, and goal-setting. These competencies significantly enrich both their personal and professional lives.

Increased Confidence

As a life coach, I assist my clients in recognizing their strengths and boosting their self-esteem. With my support, they often cultivate a stronger sense of self-confidence in their abilities.

Work-Life Balance

I am dedicated to helping my clients find a healthier balance between their work and personal lives. I guide them in setting boundaries and optimizing their time management.

Achieving Goals More Effectively

Clients frequently discover they reach their goals more quickly with my guidance. I help them formulate actionable steps and stay focused, making the journey toward progress much easier.

If you're ready to make positive changes in your life, feel free to contact me, and together we can start this transformative journey.

"You'll never change your life until you change something you do daily. The secret of your success or happiness is found in your daily routine."
– John Maxwell –

Picture courtesy of Ryan Palmieri

"Be soft. Do not let the world make you hard. Do not let the pain make you hate. Do not let the bitterness steal your sweetness. Take pride that even though the rest of the world may disagree, you still believe it to be a beautiful place."
– Kurt Vonnegut –

CURTAIN CALL

Final Thoughts and Thank You.

"We delight in the beauty of the butterfly, but rarely admit the changes it has gone through to achieve that beauty."
- Maya Angelou -

I hope you all made it to the end of my book. For those of you who are still with me, a sincere thank you and a special invitation to join me in an immersive experience to watch one of my most exciting close-up magic performances which was recorded in 360 degree Virtual reality a few years ago. I was an early adopter using this amazing technology to transport you to the best seats in the house, front row center. Feel free to move your mouse to look around to watch your fellow spectators' real time reactions to the magical moments and the jokes.

360° View of The Close-up Gallery Audience

Reprise

Some Additional Interviews

"Being an entrepreneur is a mindset. You have to see things as opportunities all the time. I like to do interviews. I like to push people on certain topics. I like to dig into the stories where there's not necessarily a right or wrong answer."
- Soledad O'Brien -

I have been interviewed by some notable names in both magic and the press. Feel free to watch me tell some of my favorite stories by clicking the QR codes below.

Epilogue

Throughout all my endeavors, triumphs and tragedies, I have maintained a single focus: To contribute positively to the world.

My aspiration as a performer, author, speaker and coach, is to ignite inspiration within you.

Life is not a race to be won, but a journey to be experienced.

In the end, we are not measured by the challenges we face, but by how bravely we face them.

You are the author, producer and star of your own show. Make it a masterpiece.

Magically Yours,

ABOUT THE AUTHOR

John Kippen Is the CEO of a successful I.T. Company, a Motivational Speaker, Success and Life Coach, Award Winning Film Producer, and now, a Published Author. He is also a World Class Magician who performs at private events and venues including Hollywood's prestigious Magic Castle.

John was dealt a bad hand; trauma left his face paralyzed and branded him negatively as "different." This life-shattering event ironically exposed his life's purpose to assist others to realize, "Being Different is Your Superpower" and how to "Feed your Heart with Your Art."

In this book, he reveals how he harnessed the power of magic to transform himself from a man who was depressed and defeated into an inspirational leader.

He currently resides in Los Angeles with his dog Carolina.

See who John has helped and discover your superpower when you visit: www.JohnKippen.com

Quotes Collection

"The hard must become habit. The habit must become easy,
The easy must become beautiful."
- Doug Henning -

"Time has a way of demonstrating that the most stubborn are
the most intelligent. "
-Yevgeny Yevtushenko -

"Snatching the eternal out of the desperately fleeting is the
great magic trick of human existence."
- Tennessee Williams -

"When you forgive, you in no way change the past - but you
sure do change the future."
- Bernard Meltzer -

"You don't have to see the whole staircase, just take the first
step."
- Martin Luther King, Jr. -

"The art of a magician is to create wonder. If we live with a
sense of wonder, our lives become filled with joy."
- Doug Henning -

"Life breaks us all but in the end we are stronger in the broken
places."
- Ernest Hemingway -

"Comebacks after surgery are not at all easy. After a major
surgery the difficult part is to conquer the inner demons. It's all
in the mind. only the individual can overcome their fears."
- Rohit Sharma -

"There is something in the human spirit that will survive and
prevail, there is a tiny and brilliant light burning in the heart of
man that will not go out no matter how dark the world
becomes."
- Leo Tolstoy -

"Hope sees the invisible, feels the intangible, and achieves the impossible."
- Helen Keller -

"The world accommodates you for fitting in, but only rewards you for standing out."
- Matshona Dhliwayo -

"You either get bitter or you get better. It's that simple. You either take what has been dealt to you and allow it to make you a better person, or you allow it to tear you down. The choice does not belong to fate, it belongs to you."
- Josh Shipp -

"Poker is a fascinating, wonderful, intricate adventure on the high seas of human nature."
- David A. Daniel -

"Magic is believing in yourself. If you can make that happen, you can make anything happen."
- Goethe -

"The face is the mirror of the mind, and eyes without speaking confess the secrets of the heart."
St. Jerome

"Every superhero needs a sidekick."
- Anonymous -

"Your time is limited, so don't waste it living someone else's life. Don't be trapped by dogma - which is living with the results of other people's thinking. Don't let the noise of other's opinions drown out your own inner voice. And most important, have the courage to follow your heart and intuition. They somehow already know what you truly want to become. Everything else is secondary."
- Steve Jobs -

"I think anything is possible if you have the mindset and the will and desire to do it and put the time in."
- Roger Clemens -

"The beautiful thing about learning is that no one can take it away from you."
- B.B. King -

"Being Different is Your Superpower."
- John David Kippen -

"There are no traffic jams along the extra mile."
- Zig Ziglar -

"Face your deficiencies and acknowledge them; but do not let them master you. Let them teach you patience, sweetness and insight."
- Helen Keller -

"Only those who will risk going too far can possibly find out how far one can go."
- T.S. Eliot -

"If there ever comes a day when we can't be together, keep me in your heart. I'll stay there forever."
- Winnie the Pooh -

"In a mystery, the sleuth must be believably involved and emotionally invested in solving the crime."
- Diane Mott Davidson -

"The reasonable man adapts himself to the world; the unreasonable one persists to adapt the world to himself. Therefore all progress depends on the unreasonable man."
- George Bernard Shaw -

"Magic is believing in yourself. If you can make that happen, you can make anything happen."
- Goethe -

"I now see how owning our story and loving ourselves through that process is the bravest thing that we will ever do."
– Brené Brown –

"The meaning of life is to find your gift. The purpose of life is to give it away."
– Pablo Picasso –

"I learned that courage was not the absence of fear, but the triumph over it. The brave man is not he who does not feel afraid, but he who conquers that fear."
– Nelson Mandela –

"Nothing in life is to be feared, it is only to be understood. Now is the time to understand more, so that we may fear less."
– Marie Curie –

"Living is the art of loving. Loving is the art of caring. Caring is the art of sharing. Sharing is the art of living. If you want to lift yourself up, lift up someone else."
– Booker T. Washington –

"Whatever you do in life, if you want to be creative and intelligent, and develop your brain, you must do everything with the awareness that everything, in some way, connects to everything else."
– Leonardo Da Vinci –

"The art of a magician is to create wonder. If we live with a sense of wonder, our lives become filled with joy."
– Doug Henning –

"Be soft. Do not let the world make you hard. Do not let the pain make you hate. Do not let the bitterness steal your sweetness. Take pride that even though the rest of the world may disagree, you still believe it to be a beautiful place."
– Kurt Vonnegut –

"There is no insurmountable solitude. All paths lead to the same goal: to convey to others what we are. And we must pass through solitude and difficulty, isolation and silence in order to reach forth to the enchanted place where we can dance our clumsy dance and sing our sorrowful song - but in this dance or in this song there are fulfilled the most ancient rites of our conscience in the awareness of being human and of believing in a common destiny." - Pablo Neruda -

"We delight in the beauty of the butterfly, but rarely admit the changes it has gone through to achieve that beauty."
- Maya Angelou -

"Never forget that you are one of a kind. Never forget that if there weren't any need for you, in all your uniqueness, to be on this earth, you wouldn't be here in the first place. And never forget, no matter how overwhelming life's challenges and problems seem to be, that one person can make a difference in the world. In fact, it is always because of one person that all the changes that matter in the world come about. So be that one person."
- R. Buckminster Fuller -

"A human being is a part of the whole called by us universe, a part limited in time and space. He experiences himself, his thoughts and feeling as something separated from the rest, a kind of optical delusion of his consciousness. This delusion is a kind of prison for us, restricting us to our personal desires and to affection for a few persons nearest to us. Our task must be to free ourselves from this prison by widening our circle of compassion to embrace all living creatures and the whole of nature in its beauty."
- Albert Einstein -

QR Code Appendix

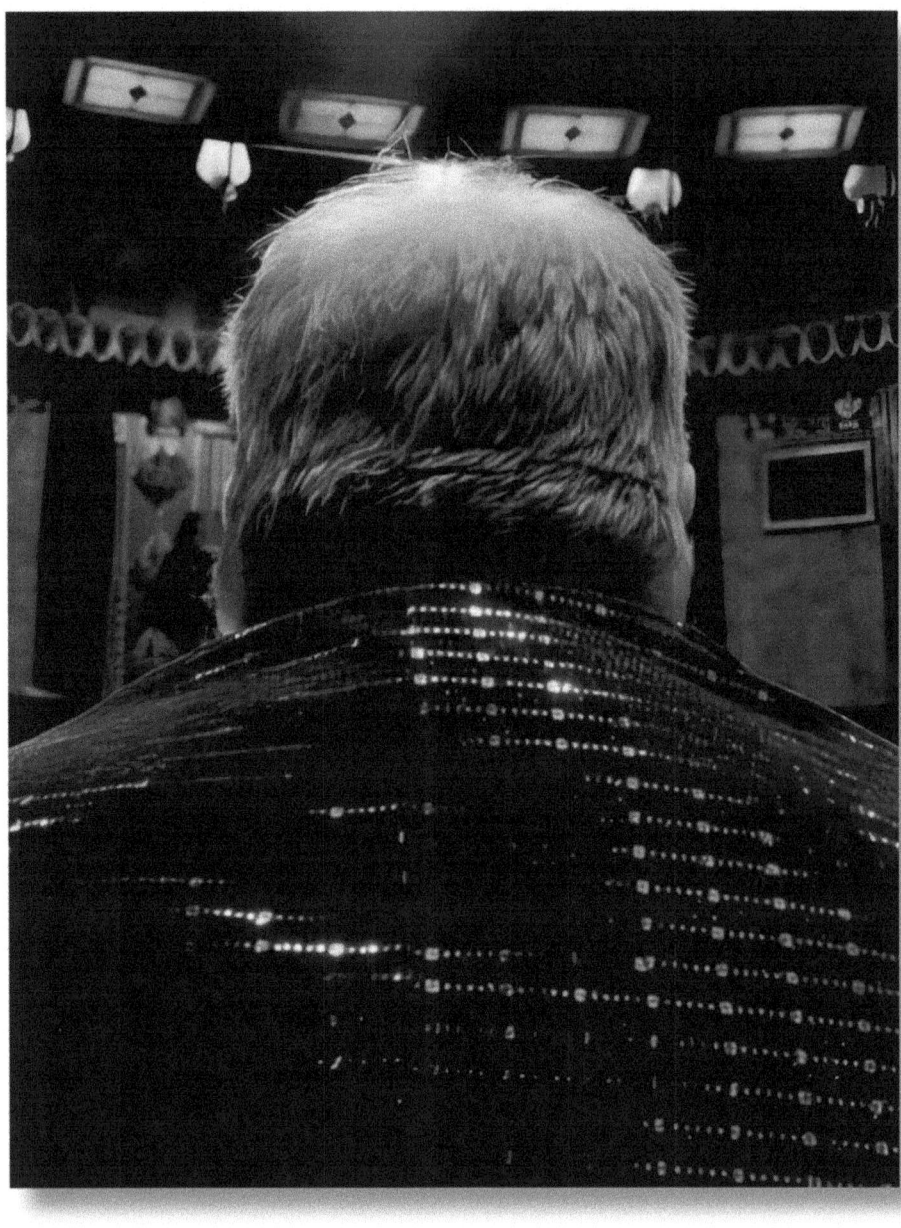

www.ingramcontent.com/pod-product-compliance
Lightning Source LLC
Chambersburg PA
CBHW051143120626
46547CB00012B/924